The Fall of the Roman Empire

The Fall of the Roman Empire

Titles in the History's Great Defeats series include:

The Aztecs: End of a Civilization
The British Empire: The End of Colonialism
The Cold War: Collapse of Communism
The Crusades: Failed Holy Wars
The French Revolution: The Fall of the Monarchy
The Indian Wars: From Frontier to Reservation
The Napoleonic Wars: Defeat of the Grand Army
The Third Reich: Demise of the Nazi Dream

HISTORY'S
GREAT DEFEATS

The Fall of the Roman Empire

by Don Nardo

LUCENT
BOOKS®

THOMSON
————★————™
GALE

San Diego • Detroit • New York • San Francisco • Cleveland
New Haven, Conn. • Waterville, Maine • London • Munich

© 2004 by Lucent Books. Lucent Books is an imprint of The Gale Group, Inc.,
a division of Thomson Learning, Inc.

Lucent Books® and Thomson Learning™ are trademarks used herein under license.

For more information, contact
Lucent Books
27500 Drake Rd.
Farmington Hills, MI 48331-3535
Or you can visit our Internet site at http://www.gale.com

LIBRARY OF CONGRESS CATALOGING-IN-PUBLICATION DATA

Nardo, Don
  The fall of the roman empire / by Don Nardo.
    v. cm. — (History's great defeats series)
  Contents: The Giant Shadow of Rome's Fall—Barbarians Overrun the Roman Realm—
Loss of Economic Stability and Security—Increasing Political and Social Disunity—
Christianity Weakens the Roman Spirit—Fatal Deterioration of the Roman Army.
   ISBN 1-59018-427-0 (hardback : alk. paper)
  I. Title. II. Series: History's great defeats (San Diego, Calif.).

Printed in the United States of America

Table of Contents

Foreword

HISTORY IS FILLED with tales of dramatic encounters that sealed the fates of empires or civilizations, changing them or causing them to disappear forever. One of the best known events began in 334 B.C., when Alexander, king of Macedonia, led his small but formidable Greek army into Asia. In the short span of only ten years, he brought Persia, the largest empire the world had yet seen, to its knees, earning him the nickname forever after associated with his name—"the Great." The demise of Persia, which at its height stretched from the shores of the Mediterranean Sea in the west to the borders of India in the east, was one of history's most stunning defeats. It occurred primarily because of some fatal flaws in the Persian military system, disadvantages the Greeks had exploited before, though never as spectacularly as they did under Alexander.

First, though the Persians had managed to conquer many peoples and bring huge territories under their control, they had failed to create an individual fighting man who could compare with the Greek hoplite. A heavily armored infantry soldier, the hoplite fought in a highly effective and lethal battlefield formation—the phalanx. Possessed of better armor, weapons, and training than the Persians, Alexander's soldiers repeatedly crushed their Persian opponents. Second, the Persians for the most part lacked generals of the caliber of their Greek counterparts. And when Alexander invaded, Persia had the added and decisive disadvantage of facing one of the greatest generals of all time. When the Persians were defeated, their great empire was lost forever.

Other world powers and civilizations have fallen in a like manner. They have succumbed to some combination of inherent fatal flaws or disadvantages, to political and/or military mistakes, and even to the personal failings of their leaders.

Another of history's great defeats was the sad demise of the North American Indian tribes at the hands of encroaching European civilization from the sixteenth to nineteenth centuries. In this case, all of the tribes suffered from the same crippling disadvantages. Among the worst, they lacked the great numbers, the unity, and the advanced industrial and military hardware possessed by the Europeans. Still another example, one closer to our own time, was the resounding defeat of Nazi Germany by the Allies in 1945, which brought World War II, the most disastrous conflict in history, to a close. Nazi Germany collapsed for many reasons. But one of the most telling was that its leader, Adolf Hitler, sorely underestimated the material resources and human resolve of the Allies, especially the United States. In the end, Germany was in a very real sense submerged by a massive and seemingly relentless tidal wave of Allied bombs, tanks, ships, and soldiers.

Seen in retrospect, a good many of the fatal flaws, drawbacks, and mistakes that caused these and other great defeats from the pages of history seem obvious. It is only natural to wonder why, in each case, the losers did not realize their limitations and/or errors sooner and attempt to avert disaster. But closer examination of the events, social and political trends, and leading personalities involved usually reveals that complex factors were at play. Arrogance, fear, ignorance, stubbornness, innocence, and other attitudes held by nations, peoples, and individuals often colored and shaped their reactions, goals, and strategies. And it is both fascinating and instructive to reconstruct how such attitudes, as well as the fatal flaws and mistakes themselves, contributed to the losers' ultimate demise.

Each volume in Lucent Books' *History's Great Defeats* series is designed to provide the reader with diverse learning tools for exploring the topic at hand. Each well-informed, clearly written text is supported and enlivened by substantial quotes by the actual people involved, as well as by later historians and other experts; and these primary and secondary sources are carefully documented. Each volume also supplies the reader with an extensive Works Consulted list, guiding him or her to further research on the topic. These and other research tools, including glossaries and time lines, afford the reader a thorough understanding of how and why one of history's most decisive defeats occurred and how these events shaped our world.

The Giant Shadow of Rome's Fall

Introduction

T he late and noted classical historian Chester G. Starr once remarked, "The best-known fact about the Roman Empire is that it declined and fell."[1] He was half-joking, of course. After all, most people know at least a few other major facts about ancient Rome. It had one of the finest armies in history, for example, and the Roman military general Julius Caesar, who conquered Gaul (what is now France), is still a household name. After another well-known event related to Caesar, his assassination in the Senate, the Roman realm continued to expand. And for many centuries, Rome ruled the entire Mediterranean world. The Romans built thousands of miles of paved roads (the source of the famous line "all roads lead to Rome"), as well as aqueducts that carried life-giving water from the countryside into cities. They erected huge amphitheaters where tens of thousands of people watched gladiators fight to the death. In addition, Rome passed along Christianity, the Latin language, and its fair and expansive law code to future generations of Europeans. Indeed, Rome provided a crucial link from Western society's dimly lit past to its better-known present. As historian Max Cary phrases it:

> Rome was the principal channel through which the modern world has entered on the heritage of the ancient. If "all roads lead to Rome," they also lead out again *from* Rome. For those who have learned to think beyond yesterday, Rome is the focusing-point of the world's history.[2]

Still, there is no escaping the fact that the Romans would not have passed on their great legacy to the modern world if the western

Roman Empire had not disintegrated and disappeared in the fifth and sixth centuries. (The eastern part of the realm, centered at Constantinople, on the southern edge of the Black Sea, mutated into the Byzantine Empire and lasted until 1453, when it fell to the Turks.) In fact, if western Rome had not fallen when it did, it might have survived for a thousand more years; it might even still be alive and well today. Either way, history would have been profoundly different in ways too numerous and complex to imagine.

For those peoples and nations that came after Rome, therefore, its fall made their rise possible. And that enormous collapse of a great

The city of Rome (looking eastward) as it appeared at its height of power and splendor in the second century A.D.

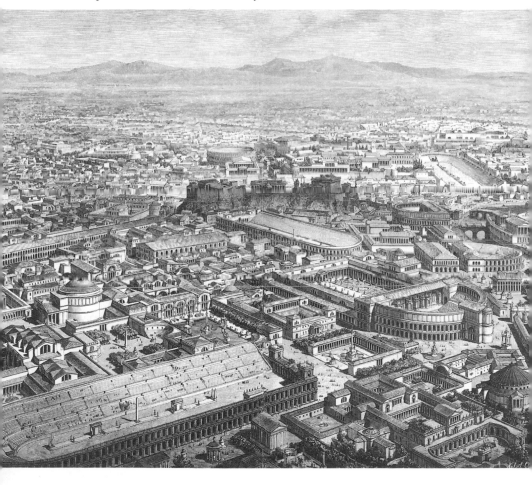

civilization continues to loom, like some giant, ominous shadow, at the dividing line between the ancient and modern eras. It is no wonder, then, that thousands of books and articles have appeared over the past few centuries trying to understand and explain what is surely one of the watershed events of history.

Gibbon's Monumental Tome

The first modern historian to launch a major study of Rome's fall was an eighteenth-century Englishman, Edward Gibbon. Between 1776 and 1788, he published the six volumes making up *The Decline and Fall of the Roman Empire.* Despite its age, it is only slightly dated, and several editions published in the twentieth century contain notes and commentary providing readers with information that has come to light since Gibbon's day. Gibbon was so great a historian, in fact, that experts still universally recognize his *Decline and Fall* as the classic work of the genre.

Even before beginning this monumental tome, Gibbon was, like other scholars of his time, aware that the so-called barbarians had overrun the Roman realm. "Barbarians" was the unflattering name the Greeks and Romans gave to the tribal peoples inhabiting central and northern Europe in ancient times. Made up mostly of Germanic and Celtic groups, these peoples had no large cities, systems of paved roads, or libraries brimming with written literature; hence Greco-Roman society viewed them as backward, sometimes even savage.

Over the long centuries of Rome's existence, some of the northern tribes made occasional and sometimes widely destructive incursions into Roman lands. But in the later years of the fourth century, these seemed like a mere trickle in comparison to the veritable torrent Rome now faced. Barbarians seized one Roman territory after another, causing the western Empire to shrink until only Italy and parts of a few nearby provinces were left. In 476, the young emperor Romulus Augustulus was forced to vacate his throne and no Roman ruler took his place. Rome had been utterly and thoroughly defeated. And there was no chance it would rise again. As the great French historian André Piganiol put it, "It is too easy to say that . . . the Roman Empire in the West was not destroyed by a brutal blow . . . that it was [only] 'sleeping.' Roman civilization did not die a natural death. It was murdered."[3]

Edward Gibbon, the English historian whose massive historical work remains the classic study of Rome's decline and fall.

A Matter of Timing?

It must also be said, however, that this murderous defeat was contingent in large degree on unfortunate timing. That is, the onrush of the greatest tide of barbarians occurred at a time when Rome had already been significantly weakened by internal problems and challenges. Gibbon addressed some of these in his masterwork. Rome was guilty of

The Germanic leader Arminius leads his soldiers home in triumph after ambushing and defeating a Roman army in A.D. 9.

"immoderate greatness," he said; in other words, it became too massive and complex to govern itself efficiently and safely. At the same time, political corruption and economic problems ravaged the government and hindered efficient administration of the provinces. Gibbon also cited the rise of Christianity, saying that its pacifistic ideas weakened Rome's traditional martial spirit. "The clergy successfully preached the doctrines of patience and [cowardice]," he wrote.

> The active virtues of society [such as personal ambition and the military arts] were discouraged; and the last remains of military spirit were buried in the cloister [monastery]. A large portion of public and private wealth was consecrated to . . . [Christian] charity and devotion; and the soldiers' pay was [reduced and diverted to causes that promoted] the merits of abstinence and chastity.[4]

Later scholars suggested more factors contributing to Rome's decline and fall. These included a devaluation of money and deterioration of agriculture; the division of the Empire into two parts, each weaker than the former whole; tension and fighting between society's upper and lower classes; the moral and economic ravages of slavery; and the steady decline of the Roman army, which grew increasingly less capable of stopping the barbarian invaders. Advocating the importance of the latter factor, historian Arther Ferrill points out:

> At the opening of the fifth century a massive army, perhaps more than 200,000 strong, stood at the service of the Western emperor and his generals. In 476, it was gone. The destruction of Roman military power in the fifth century A.D. was the obvious cause of the collapse of Roman government in the West.[5]

By contrast, if the barbarian invasions had happened earlier, when the Empire was more unified, more economically sound, and guarded by a tougher, more disciplined army, the Romans may well have been able to fend off the attacks. According to this view, the barbarians defeated Rome, but they did so with the indirect (and certainly unintentional) aid of the Romans themselves. In tracing the causes for Rome's ultimate defeat, therefore, one must logically begin by examining the barbarians and the increasing threat they posed to the Empire over the centuries. But one must also consider the major factors that weakened the Roman realm during those same centuries and thereby ensured that the barbarians would succeed.

Barbarians Overrun the Roman Realm

Chapter 1

The keys to success for the barbarian tribes that overran the faltering Roman realm in the fifth century were time, great numbers, and persistence. To date, no historian has summarized it better than Edward Gibbon in his classic *Decline and Fall of the Roman Empire.* The northern regions of Europe, he wrote, "were filled with innumerable tribes of hunters and shepherds." These peoples were "bold in arms, and impatient to ravish the fruits of industry." Moreover, this "endless column of barbarians" was relentless in its attacks. If the leading tribe was defeated or halted, "the vacant space was instantly replenished by new assailants."[6] In this way, the barbarians steadily wore the Romans down until resistance was ultimately futile and the Empire had been permanently defeated and dismembered.

The question is whether or not this dire outcome was inevitable. And the answer depends on which point in Roman history one begins to examine the problem of the northern barbarians. The fact is that the invasions that began in the late fourth century and brought about Rome's fall a century later were not the first major encounter between Roman civilization and Germanic-Celtic civilization. Smaller-scale barbarian incursions had plagued the Greco-Roman world off and on for many centuries. Had the Romans dealt with these assailants in a decisive manner earlier, the invasions of the fifth century would have been much smaller (if they happened at all) and Rome may well have survived them. As a brief examination of Roman-barbarian relations reveals, however, when Rome was at its strongest it rarely went fully on the offensive against its northern neighbors; instead, with one notable exception, it remained always on the defensive. This allowed the barbarians to grow increasingly numerous and powerful until their success against the Romans was assured.

The Endless Column of Barbarians

The following excerpt, from his renowned *Decline and Fall of the Roman Empire,* is Edward Gibbon's eloquent and often-quoted general statement about the onslaught of the northern barbarians.

Beyond the Rhine and Danube [rivers] the northern countries of Europe and Asia were filled with innumerable tribes of hunters and shepherds, poor, voracious, and turbulent; bold in arms, and impatient to ravish the fruits of industry. The barbarian world was agitated by the rapid impulse of war; and the peace of Gaul or Italy was shaken by the distant revolutions of China. The Huns, who fled before a victorious enemy, directed their march toward the West; and the torrent was swelled by the gradual accession of captives and allies. The flying tribes who yielded to the Huns assumed in *their* turn the spirit of conquest; the endless column of barbarians pressed on the Roman Empire with accumulated weight; and if the foremost were destroyed, the vacant space was instantly replenished by new assailants.

A Germanic tribe on the move. So-called "barbarian" tribes threatened Rome many times over the centuries.

Early Encounters with Gauls and Germans

Eerily, the first major Roman encounter with the barbarians was nearly eight centuries before the final one, and hauntingly similar to it in many ways. At the start of the fourth century B.C., Rome was one of several strong city-states occupying west-central Italy. The Romans still had a republican form of government in which a citizen assembly elected public officials, including two jointly serving consuls, who administered the state and commanded the army. Most governmental power, however, rested in the Senate, whose members were all wealthy and served for life.

In 390 B.C., the consuls and senators found themselves facing a crucial decision. A few years before, a force of Gauls (the name given by the Greeks and Romans to Celts who occupied what are now Switzerland, France, and Belgium) had descended from the Alps into northern Italy. The intruders overran that region and some of them settled there. Then, early in 390, a large force of Gallic warriors began marching southward, sacking Italian towns and villages as they went. Eventually, they threatened Roman territory. With the Gauls fast approaching, the consuls mustered the Roman army, which was still a part-time militia force made up of farmers and laborers who assembled to fight a battle and then returned to their jobs as soon as it was over.

Thus, most of the Roman troops who met the invaders near the Allia River were inexperienced. They also had never before seen a barbarian army. Suddenly they were face to face with thousands of tribal warriors either clad in animal skins or nearly naked, and sporting shoulder-length hair and war paint. Wasting no time, the Gauls attacked, screaming loud war cries. And the Roman ranks dissolved in panic and confusion. After their victory, the invaders occupied Rome briefly and then returned to northern Italy.

At the time, the Romans lacked the manpower and other means to strike back at the Gauls in their own homeland. So Rome simply absorbed the lessons of its defeat and moved on. One lesson the Romans learned was that they must be better prepared to meet future military threats, and to this end, they instituted major military reforms that over time gave them the most powerful army in the Mediterranean sphere. This army served them well when the Cimbri and Teutones, two large Germanic tribes, threatened Italy in the late second century

The Romans Flee at Allia

The first-century-B.C. Roman historian Livy describes the panic of the Roman soldiers at Allia in 390 B.C. in this passage from his history of Rome (excerpted here from Aubrey de Sélincourt's translation in *Livy: The Early History of Rome*).

> In the lines of the legionaries [Roman soldiers]—officers and men alike—there was no trace of the old Roman manhood. They fled in panic, so blinded by everything but saving their skins that, in spite of the fact that the Tiber [River] lay in their way, most of them tried to get to Veii, once an enemy town, instead of making for their own homes in Rome. . . . The main body of the army, at the first sound of the Gallic war-cry . . . hardly waited even to see their strange enemy from the ends of the earth; they made no attempt at resistance . . . but fled before they had lost a single man. . . . Near the bank of the river there was a terrible slaughter; the whole left wing of the army had gone that way and had flung away their arms in the desperate hope of getting over. Many could not swim and many others in their exhausted state were dragged under . . . and drowned.

Gallic warriors drive Roman troops into the Allia River in 390 B.C. Rome never forgot the "dark day of Allia."

B.C. (By this time, the Roman Republic controlled the entire peninsula, as well as most of the lands bordering the Mediterranean.) Between 109 and 106 B.C., the Germans defeated several small Roman forces sent against them and entered northern Italy. But then Rome's greatest living general, Gaius Marius, entered the fray and crushed the intruders.

One of many modern artistic renderings of the Gallic chief and hero Vercingetorix surrendering to Julius Caesar.

Unlike his forebears who fought at Allia, Marius had the men and resources to carry the war to the enemy's homeland. He could have led troops into central Europe and created a Roman-controlled buffer zone to keep the northern Roman borders safer. But for reasons unknown, he and the Roman government apparently did not seriously consider such a plan. They seem to have assumed that the decisive defeat of the Cimbri and Teutones would be an ample deterrent against future barbarian incursions.

Caesar's Success; Augustus's Failure

One Roman military leader who reversed this defensive strategy and went on the offensive against the barbarians was Marius's nephew (by marriage), Julius Caesar. In his capacity as governor of two Roman provinces on the fringe of barbarian territory, Cisalpine Gaul (northern Italy) and Narbonese Gaul (southern France), Caesar raised troops for a major undertaking. His goal was to conquer Transalpine Gaul, the then little-known region comprising what are now western Switzerland, central and northern France, and the Netherlands and Belgium. Beginning in 58 B.C., he led campaign after campaign against the tribal peoples of this region. And eight years later, most of barbarian Gaul had been pacified. In the century that followed, its peoples became Romanized as they adopted Roman customs and the Latin language; and the provinces set up in Gaul proved to be among the most prosperous and productive in the Roman realm.

Modern observers have often criticized Caesar for his aggressive methods and seemingly unprovoked attacks on the Gallic tribes. From the ancient Roman standpoint, however, his conquests opened up important new lands and resources for the Romans to exploit. Caesar also ensured the security of the realm's northwestern borders by bringing a former barbarian region directly into the Roman fold.

At first, it seemed as though Caesar's eventual successor, his adopted son Octavian, would carry this same strategy into the Germanic-held lands of central and eastern Europe. After Caesar's assassination in 44 B.C., the young Octavian battled several rivals for control of the Roman realm. A long series of civil wars had already brought the Republic's traditional government to its knees. And after Octavian emerged victorious from the last of these conflicts in 31 B.C., he established a new, more autocratic form of government.

Renamed Augustus (the "revered one"), Octavian became the first
ruler of the political entity that came to be called the Roman Empire.

The problem of what to do about the northern German tribes became
the centerpiece of Augustus's foreign policy. Some German tribes controlled territories lying only two hundred miles north of the Roman
heartland in Italy. And like other Roman leaders, he felt that the close
proximity of these barbarians was dangerous and intolerable. Augustus reasoned that pushing the realm's northern border about 150 miles
farther north, to the Danube River, would better keep the barbarians at
bay. So he ordered his generals to begin moving northward into German lands. By 15 B.C., these efforts had succeeded in making the Danube
Rome's northern border, and four new provinces were established in
the newly conquered lands.

The Danube frontier did not remain quiet, however, as Augustus
had hoped it would. German raiding parties became a problem, and he
responded by sending troops past the Danube into the German heartland, the territory lying between the Rhine, Danube, and Elbe rivers.
This approach seemed to work, because in the years that followed Germany remained relatively quiet. So, Augustus decided the time was
ripe to begin pacifying and Romanizing the Germans, as Rome was
already doing to the Gauls.

To this end, the emperor sent a former consul, Publius Quintilius
Varus, to deal with the natives and organize a new province. Unfortu-
nately, Varus was conceited and tactless and ended up alienating the
Germans, many of whom had actually begun to welcome the idea of
becoming Romans. To get revenge on Varus, a large German force
attacked him in A.D. 9 in the Teutoburg Forest (about eighty miles
east of the Rhine). Varus and nearly all of his fifteen thousand troops
were killed.

To the Brink of Collapse and Back

Usually a calm and collected individual, Augustus reacted to the news
of the catastrophe with violent emotion. According to the first-century-
A.D. Roman historian Suetonius: "It is said that he took the disaster
so deeply to heart that he left his hair and beard untrimmed for months;
he would often beat his head on a door, shouting: 'Quintilius Varus,
give me back my legions!'"[7] Not only could Varus not give the legions

Varus and his men are slaughtered in the Teutoburg Forest. After this defeat, Augustus withdrew the remainder of his forces from Germany.

back, but completely replacing them and their weapons would have bankrupted the emperor. Discouraged, Augustus wrote off Germany as a loss and withdrew the remainder of his forces from the German heartland, which allowed the natives to regain control of the area.

No one at the time realized that, because of Augustus's failure to follow up on Varus's defeat, Rome's best chance of absorbing and Romanizing the Germans had passed by. Perhaps the next best chance came in the following century. In 166 a group of Germanic tribes led by the Marcomanni attacked Rome's northern borders. In two bloody wars, the emperor Marcus Aurelius managed, with great difficulty, to push the invaders back. He eventually had them at his mercy. And apparently he planned to maintain his momentum and absorb their homelands. However, in March 180 Aurelius died, leaving his far less responsible and visionary son Commodus in control of the Empire. In an effort to appease the Marcomanni and other Germans, Commodus struck deals with them and made no attempt to invade their territories; thus, once more, the natives were left to regroup in preparation for another round of attacks on Rome.

That round began in the 230s when a large Germanic group, the Goths, raided Rome's northern border provinces. In 251 the invaders defeated and killed the emperor Decius and then split into two groups: the Ostrogoths and Visigoths, each of which remained a menace. Meanwhile, the success of the Goths emboldened other northern tribes. In 260 the Alamanni penetrated northern Italy and other tribes invaded Gaul and Spain. By this time, economic and other internal problems had caused the Empire to grow weak, and at times the combination of external threats and internal crises caused the Roman government to teeter on the brink of collapse. As noted historian Michael Grant puts it, "It seemed as if the Roman world . . . could not possibly survive." Yet seemingly miraculously, the Romans, who had many times before proved themselves a remarkably resilient people, managed to avoid annihilation. Beginning in the year 268, a series of strong and effective soldier-emperors emerged and "in one of the most striking reversals in world history," says Grant, "Rome's foes were hurled back."[8]

The Huns, Visigoths, and Adrianople

The strongest of these soldier-emperors, Diocletian (reigned 284–305), established what was in effect a new Roman realm, which modern historians often call the Later Empire. During Diocletian's watch and

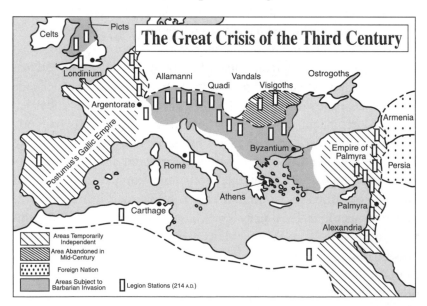

The Great Crisis of the Third Century

those of his immediate successors, the northern borders were relatively quiet. But this silence was deceptive. As they had in the past, during the period of calm the barbarians grew in numbers and some became increasingly restive. It was only a matter of time before some event would cause them to go on the move once again and threaten the integrity of Rome's borders.

That event occurred in about 370, when a warlike nomadic people from central Asia—the Huns—swept into eastern Europe. The Huns appeared repulsive and frightening even to the Germanic barbarians, which is not surprising considering the description of these Asian warriors given by the fourth-century Roman historian Ammianus Marcellinus. They "are quite abnormally savage," he wrote, "and are so prodigiously ugly and bent that they might be two-legged animals." The Huns did not cook their food, Ammianus said, "but live on the roots of wild plants and the half-raw flesh of any sort of animals, which they warm a little by placing it between their thighs and the backs of their horses."[9]

These "abnormally savage" Huns quickly destroyed the kingdom the Ostrogoths had recently established in what is now Ukraine. The invaders also forced more than 200,000 terrified Visigoths across the Danube into Roman territory. The emperor Valens permitted these refugees to settle down. (Valens was ruler of the eastern sector of the realm; following a tradition begun by Diocletian, an eastern emperor ruled from Asia Minor and a western one from Italy, although the Empire was still technically a single entity.) It is likely that welcoming the intruders was a selfish move on Valens's part, as he hoped to recruit Visigothic fighters for his army.

The deal fell through, however, when the emperor's agents unwisely insulted and tried to exploit the Visigoths. The tribesmen reacted by looting much of the province of Thrace (north of Greece), which forced Valens to lead troops against them. The headstrong ruler made the mistake of attacking before his nephew, the western emperor Gratian, could arrive with extra soldiers. On August 9, 378, the overconfident Valens and as many as forty thousand of his men were slaughtered at Adrianople, in Thrace. Ammianus's riveting account of the battle reads in part:

Amid the clashing of arms and weapons on every side . . . sounding the death-knell of the Roman cause, our retreating

Ammianus on the Huns

In this excerpt from his chronicle of Rome, the fourth-century Roman historian Ammianus Marcellinus describes the invading Huns.

[The Huns] are quite abnormally savage. . . . They have squat bodies, strong limbs, and thick necks, and are so prodigiously ugly and bent that they might be two-legged animals, or the figures [gargoyles] crudely carved from stumps which are seen on the parapets of bridges. . . . Their way of life is so rough that they have no use for fire or seasoned food, but live on the roots of wild plants and the half-raw flesh of any sort of animals, which they warm a little by placing it between their thighs and the backs of their horses. They have no buildings to shelter them, but avoid anything of the kind as carefully as we avoid living in the neighborhood of tombs. . . . Once they have put their necks into some dingy shirt they never take it off or change it till it rots and falls to pieces. . . . When they join battle they advance in packs, uttering their various war-cries. Being lightly equipped and very sudden in their movements they can deliberately scatter and gallop about at random, inflicting tremendous slaughter.

A modern drawing captures the ferocity and savagery of the Huns, who drove the Germans into Roman lands.

troops rallied with shouts of mutual encouragement. But, as the fighting spread like fire and numbers of them were transfixed by arrows and whirling javelins, they lost heart. Then the opposing lines came into collision like ships of war and pushed each other to and fro, heaving under the reciprocal motion like the waves of the sea. . . . Dust rose in such clouds as to hide the sky, which rang with frightful shouts. . . . The barbarians poured on in huge columns, trampling down horse and man and crushing our ranks so as to make an orderly retreat impossible. Our men were too close-packed to have any hope of escape; so they resolved to die like heroes, faced the enemy's swords, and struck back at their assailants. [10]

Federate Status: An Ominous Precedent

By "death-knell of the Roman cause," Ammianus meant Rome's short-term loss in the struggle against the Visigoths. At the time, he had no way of knowing that the phrase also foreshadowed the longer-term Roman slide into oblivion that began with this crippling defeat. First, the Roman government was never able to replace all of the soldiers who perished at Adrianople. And the defeat also had a negative psychological effect on the Roman populace, who thereafter grew increasingly uneasy about the future.

At the same time, the folk migrations the Huns had set in motion were just beginning. In the years immediately following Adrianople, Europe was thrown into an enormous state of chaos. Dozens of Germanic and Celtic tribes, among them the Burgundians, Franks, Vandals, Angles, and Alani, were driven from their lands and struck out in search of new ones. Some, in their turn, dispossessed other tribes, which then poured across Roman borders. These population movements completely dwarfed any that Rome, or the world, had witnessed in the past. As time went on, the Romans offered military resistance when and where they could. But overall the problem was too widespread and the numbers of intruders too huge to deal with strictly on a military basis.

As an alternative, in what amounted to a desperate attempt to stave off disaster, the Roman government began to make accommodations with the intruders. The first major example occurred in 382, when

The emperor Theodosius meets with Visigothic leaders. Theodosius allowed the Visigoths to settle in Roman territory.

Theodosius, who succeeded the unfortunate Valens, negotiated a deal with the Visigoths. He permitted them to settle in Thrace permanently, free from taxation. All they had to do was provide a yearly quota of troops for the Roman army. The Visigoths were even allowed to more or less govern themselves in their own territory, making them "federates," or equal allies living within the Empire.

The precedent this deal set for Rome's future was ominous to say the least. It marked the first time that a portion of the Roman realm was no longer under direct Roman control. Indeed, in the years that followed, other tribes negotiated federate status for themselves and carved out their own personal niches in the western provinces. One obvious negative outcome for the Roman government was that it lost much of its authority over an increasing amount of territory. Yet the emperors felt they had no choice but to continue the policy. They lacked the resources to fight all the barbarian groups entering the realm, and they became increasingly dependent on barbarian troops to replenish the ranks of the Roman army.

The Barbarian Eclipse

One dire need for these fresh troops was to help put down rebellions by imperial usurpers, who plagued the realm in the late fourth and early fifth centuries. In 392, for example, a general named Arbogast ordered the murder of the western emperor, Valentinian II, and placed a prominent public official, Eugenius, on the throne. Theodosius, who still controlled the Empire's eastern sector, decided to act. He marched a large army, which included some twenty thousand Visigoths, to northeastern Italy. In a hard-fought battle waged in 394 near the Frigidus River, he defeated the claimants and executed Eugenius. (Arbogast fled and committed suicide.) Theodosius's barbarian troops proved crucial in the victory, as he placed them in the forefront of his army when he attacked.

Barbarian troops proved to be fearless and effective fighters. However, Germans and other tribesmen lacked the cultural roots and loyalty to Rome and its ideals that native Romans possessed. So barbarian

A band of Huns pillages a villa in the Roman countryside. Led by Attila, the Huns were finally defeated in 451.

allies could be fickle and unpredictable. The Visigoths themselves demonstrated this shortly after their mentor, Theodosius, died in 395 and his sons, Honorius and Arcadius, became emperors in the West and East, respectively. Evidently the Visigoths did not trust these young rulers, and the relationship between the tribe and the Roman government swiftly soured. In 402, led by their capable general Alaric, they marched on Italy. But their advance was temporarily halted by Honorius's own barbarian general, Stilicho.

These developments set in motion a series of events that did not bode well for Rome. To deal with the Visigoths, Honorius unwisely recalled most of the Roman troops stationed in the province of Britain. Left largely unguarded, Britain rapidly succumbed to attacks by hostile barbarian groups, including the Picts and Saxons. Meanwhile, armies of Vandals, Alani, and Suevi invaded Gaul and Rome's Spanish provinces, encountering little resistance. Finally, Alaric regrouped

Under Alaric, the Visigoths enter Rome in 410. The sack of the city, symbol of Roman power, shocked the known world.

his forces and marched on Rome, which was sacked (for the first time in nearly eight hundred years) in 410.

After this outrage, what was left of the western Roman realm continued to disintegrate at an alarming rate. In the 430s, a particularly brutal and ambitious Hunnish leader, Attila, arose and in the next two decades ravaged various Roman provinces. He was defeated in 451 by an alliance of Romans and German federates near Chalons (in northeastern Gaul). But only four years later the city of Rome was sacked once more, this time by the Vandals. From this point on, the last few western emperors were all weak, ineffectual rulers whose realm consisted only of the Italian peninsula and portions of a few nearby provinces. Most power rested not with them but with their army generals, who were nearly all of German ancestry.

It was one of these generals, Odoacer, who led his men into Ravenna (which had replaced Rome as the western capital) in 476 and deposed Romulus Augustulus, the last western Roman emperor. Odoacer's troops proclaimed him king of Italy. And as Augustulus went into permanent retirement, the western imperial government, which had been barely functioning for decades, simply ceased to exist. The "accumulated weight,"[11] as Gibbon put it, of time, numbers, and sheer persistence had produced an outcome that Marius, Caesar, Augustus, and Marcus Aurelius would have deemed unthinkable—the barbarian eclipse of Rome.

Loss of

Economic Stability
Chapter 2
and Security

T he Roman Empire reached its height in size, power, and magnificence in the second century A.D., when it was easily the strongest political unit on Earth. If it had remained this strong, it is possible that it might have weathered the storm of the barbarian invasions of the late fourth and fifth centuries. But the power and stability that Rome enjoyed at its height were not destined to last. Various problems began to undermine and weaken the foundations of the realm, especially its economy, which over time suffered from the effects of a number of negative factors and developments. Among these were almost incessant warfare, a rise in lawlessness, a decline in agriculture and trade, frequent devaluation of money until it was almost worthless, excessive taxation, and depopulation and wastage of many once prosperous regions.

As in all ages, it was the poor and underprivileged who suffered most from these adverse conditions. The rich, who made up a tiny fraction of the population, were only marginally affected. The lowest classes of society made up the vast bulk of the population, and their increasing struggles to sustain the mere basic necessities of life were a symptom of a fatally ill and flawed economic system. Sooner or later, that system was bound to collapse. At the time, no one foresaw this inevitability, since the average person assumed that Rome would continue to exist forever. Yet millions knew the system was unfair and corrupt and longed for some kind of reform or reckoning. The most pious members of society believed that the reckoning might be some form of penalty meted out by God. For example, the Roman Christian priest Salvian, born about the year 400, warned:

Do we think we are unworthy of the punishment of divine severity when we thus constantly punish the poor? Do we think, when we are constantly wicked, that God should not exercise His justice against all of us? Where or in whom are evils so great, except among the Romans? [12]

On the Eve of Decline

The severity of Rome's economic decline cannot be truly appreciated without a basic understanding of the high level of prosperity the realm attained in the years immediately preceding the start of its downward spiral. In this respect, one need look no further than the reigns of the emperors Nerva, Trajan, Hadrian, Antoninus Pius, and Marcus Aurelius, who ruled consecutively between 96 and 180. Because they were such enlightened leaders and also because Rome's political and economic stability reached its height during their watch, history came to call them the "five good emperors." Gibbon best summed up their collective achievement with these now famous words:

> If a man were called upon to fix the period in the history of the world during which the condition of the human race was most happy and prosperous, he would without hesitation name that which elapsed from the [accession of Nerva to the

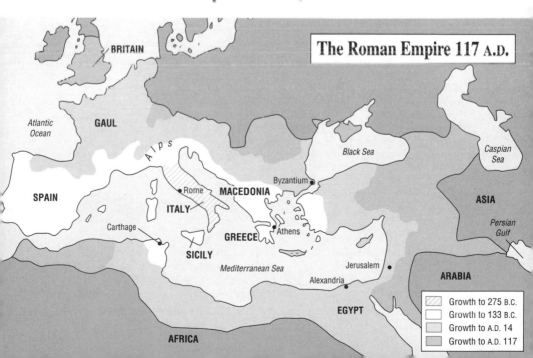

The Roman Empire 117 A.D.

BRITAIN

Atlantic Ocean

GAUL

Alps

SPAIN

Rome • MACEDONIA
ITALY

Carthage •
GREECE • Athens
SICILY

Mediterranean Sea

Black Sea

Byzantium •

ASIA

Caspian Sea

Persian Gulf

Jerusalem •
Alexandria •

ARABIA

EGYPT

AFRICA

Growth to 275 B.C.
Growth to 133 B.C.
Growth to A.D. 14
Growth to A.D. 117

death of Aurelius]. . . . Their united reigns are possibly the only period of history in which the happiness of a great people was the sole object of government. [13]

This statement is only mildly exaggerated. Under Trajan, the Empire reached its greatest geographical size—roughly 3.5 million square miles. This included not only Italy and Greece and nearby islands but also what are now Spain, France, Britain, Switzerland, Bosnia, Romania, Turkey, Armenia, Syria, Palestine, western Iraq, Egypt, Libya, Tunisia, and Morocco. Moreover, the Roman government administered this mighty realm with a sure hand. It spent vast sums on building road systems, aqueducts, temples, courts of law, and entertainment facilities. It also stationed garrisons of soldiers in every province, not only to keep the borders safe but also to discourage pirates and brigands. This increased security, which helped promote travel, trade,

Rome's main Forum, as it looked when the Empire was at its height under the "five good emperors."

and the exchange of culture and ideas. The following tract composed by Aelius Aristides, a second-century Greek writer, captured the breadth of the Roman achievement:

> Every place is full of gymnasia, fountains, gateways, temples, shops, and schools. . . . Gifts never stop flowing from you to the cities . . . [which] shine in radiance and beauty. . . . Only those outside your Empire, if there are any, are fit to be pitied for losing such blessings. . . . Greek and [non-Greek] can now readily go wherever they please with their property or without it. . . . You have surveyed the whole world, built bridges of all sorts across rivers, cut down mountains to make paths for chariots, filled the deserts with hostels, and civilized it all with system and order. [14]

It should be noted that Aristides was a well-to-do orator who reaped personal benefits from heaping praises on, and ignoring the faults of, his Roman masters. Still, his words were true in essence; in his day, Rome was, without question, the wealthiest, most prosperous, most culturally diverse, and safest major realm that had ever existed.

The Anarchy

Aristides had no way of knowing that the prosperous, pleasant world he knew had reached a peak it would never again attain. One sign of changing times was the shattering of the Empire's long era of peace and plenty when barbarians breached the borders during the reign of Marcus Aurelius. Aurelius did manage to push the invaders back and restore overall security. But then he died and his corrupt and brutal son Commodus ascended the throne. Not only did Commodus waste large sums from the public treasury on his own luxuries and other dubious projects, but he allowed corruption to flourish among his subordinates.

Although Commodus was assassinated before the Empire suffered major damage, his reign was followed by a period of civil war and political and economic uncertainty. To finance military operations and keep themselves safe from their rivals, emperors and governors raised taxes. And in the next few decades, the realm's economy began showing signs of strain. Poverty increased, which caused farming and trade to decline. Also, standard coins began to lose their value because the imperial mints encountered shortages of silver and gold and increasingly turned out coins made of cheaper metal alloys. With the currency devalued, fewer and fewer people could afford to buy essential items, let alone luxury goods.

With a sustained period of strong, enlightened leadership of the caliber of the five good emperors, these destructive trends might well have been reversed. However, the emperors of the early third century were all self-serving, corrupt individuals who were out of touch with their subjects and had little or no idea about how to administer an empire. As a result, economic conditions continued to worsen. Following the short reign of Alexander Severus (222–235), the Empire entered a roughly fifty-year period of misrule, chaos, war, and uncertainty that modern scholars often call the Anarchy. More than fifty men, usually referred to collectively as the "soldier-emperors," claimed the throne in these years, most illegally, and all but one died by assassination or other violent means.

The Anarchy almost destroyed the Empire. Barbarian armies threatened the northern provinces, while competing Roman emperors and generals fought each other as well as the invaders. Trade was disrupted, piracy became rampant, and large sectors of the populace were severely affected by poverty and crime. At the same time, the coinage became almost completely worthless. As a result, generals often lacked the money to pay their troops, who made up for this shortfall by looting Roman farms and cities.

Indeed, at times the destruction wrought by Roman soldiers was as bad as or worse than that perpetrated by the barbarians they periodically fought. Not surprisingly, civilians suffered doubly. As noted scholar A.H.M. Jones puts it:

> The combined effect of frequent devastation and looting, both by Roman armies and by barbarian hordes, and of wholesale requisitioning [official seizure] of crops and cattle . . . was disastrous to agriculture, the basic industry of the Roman Empire. Peasants deserted their holdings, either drifting to the towns, where they could pick up a living in luxury trades . . . or becoming outlaws and brigands. Large hordes of these ravaged Gaul in the latter years of the third century. [15]

Romans Prey on Romans

Herodian, a second-century-A.D. historian, penned this description (quoted in Lewis and Reinhold's *Roman Civilization, Sourcebook II*) of Roman soldiers pillaging the northern Italian city of Aquileia during the Anarchy.

> Finding the houses of the suburbs deserted, [the soldiers] cut down all the vines and trees, set some on fire, and made a shambles of the once-thriving countryside. . . . After destroying all this to the root, the army pressed on to the walls . . . and strove to demolish at least some part of the walls, so that they might break in and sack everything, razing the city and leaving the land a deserted pasturage.

Slaves of the Soil

Jones's reference to peasants deserting their lands raises the issue of declining agriculture as a major factor in Rome's continuing economic deterioration. Large tracts of once fertile land not only were abandoned by their owners but became overgrown with weeds and trees, dried out from decreasing rainfall, or eroded and became worthless for other reasons. In the western Empire's last three centuries, for example, increasing amounts of land that had once been used to grow grain and vegetables were converted into pastures for sheep and goats. "This was bad in two respects," one modern scholar writes.

> In the first place, sheep and goats eat not only grass, but seedling trees, and thus prevent the growth of new forests. Where they pasture in abundance the soil is badly trampled, and is no longer held in place by roots. Hence it is washed away by the winter rain, leaving the hillsides barren and ruining the fields in the lowlands. In the second place, sheepraising and cattle-raising demand large areas. Hence they increase the tendency toward the concentration of land in the hands of a few individuals. [16]

This tendency for a few rich individuals to take over the lands once owned by thousands of small independent farmers had actually begun long before. In the first few centuries of the Republic, many small farmers owned their own land. An average plot consisted of two to five

This nineteenth-century engraving shows Roman farmers who raise sheep and goats rather than grow crops.

acres. Over time, however, increasing numbers of small farmers were unable to compete with huge farming estates, each covering hundreds or even thousands of acres and exploiting the labor of virtual armies of slaves. These estates, known as *latifundia,* were owned by rich absentee landlords who lived in splendid houses in the cities. Some of the poor farmers who were driven out of business by the big estates migrated to Rome and other cities in search of work. Many others became poor tenant farmers who worked small sections of the estates in exchange for a modest share of the harvest.

Once this process of consolidating many small landholdings into a few larger ones was firmly established, it began to exploit the free workers on the large estates. Many of them became financially dependent on their employers, who often attempted to keep the workers and their

Binding Tenant Farmers to the Soil

This law regarding the status of *coloni* (quoted in Lewis and Reinhold's *Roman Civilization, Sourcebook II*) was passed during the reign of Constantine I.

> Any person whatsoever in whose possession a *colonus* belonging to another is found not only shall restore the said *colonus* to his place of origin, but shall also assume the . . . tax on him for the time [that he had him]. And as for *coloni* themselves, it will be proper for such as contemplate flight to be bound with chains to a servile status, so that . . . they may be compelled to fulfill the duties that befit free men.

Poor tenant farmers labor on a wealthy estate. Eventually, large numbers of agricultural workers became serfs.

descendants in the same jobs for generations. Such dependent farm-workers became known as *coloni*. "Their condition was halfway between that of freemen and that of slaves," historian Arthur Boak explains.

> While they were bound to the estates upon which they resided and passed with it from one owner to another, they were not absolutely under the power of the owner and could not be disposed of [sold] by him apart from the land. They had also other rights which slaves lacked, yet as time went on their condition tended to approximate more and more to servitude. [17]

The manner in which the estate owners controlled and often abused the *coloni* was sanctioned by a series of laws passed over the years. One law enacted in the early fourth century stated that "it will be proper for such [*coloni*] as contemplate flight to be bound with chains to a servile status, so that . . . they may be compelled to fulfill the duties that befit free men." [18] A few decades later an even harsher law ordained that *coloni* should

> be considered like slaves of the land itself to which they are born, and shall have no right of going off when they like or of changing their place, but the landowner shall enjoy his right over them with the care of a parent and the power of a master. [19]

As more and more poor Romans became such "slaves of the soil," a large percentage of the Later Empire's population became emotionally and intellectually depressed and increasingly less productive. This process contributed to the ruin of Rome's once prosperous land-based economy and fatally weakened the realm.

Efforts to Keep Prices Down

In fact, the deterioration of the economy continued, at varying rates and with some fluctuations, even after the Anarchy ended. Not long after Diocletian restored political stability and relative security in the 280s, he and his successors tried to improve the Empire's financial situation as well. The accumulated problems were simply too huge and complicated, however. A brief summary of these well-meaning efforts shows that it was already beyond the ability of the government to halt the progress of economic decay.

Diocletian's first attempted economic reform was designed to deal with the near worthlessness of money. Devaluation of the currency had

caused high inflation (rapid, steep in-
creases in the prices of goods and services), a lowered standard of living, and
widespread poverty. To stabilize the
money supply, Diocletian ordered the
minting of pure gold and silver coins.
Supplies of these precious metals were
still very limited, however, so the few
valuable coins that were circulated were
quickly snatched up by those who could
afford them and hidden in private coin
hordes. The result was that the government had no choice but to continue
to pay the army and its creditors with
devalued coins. And prices remained abnormally high. (A later emperor, Constantine I, tried a similar approach. He
issued a gold coin called the *solidus,* but
as Grant points out, this coin helped only
the well-to-do and "was of little use to
the vast majority of the inhabitants of
the Empire, who rarely if ever possessed

*A bust of the emperor Diocletian,
who instituted a number of
economic reforms that failed.*

a gold coin at all." The average person dealt only in cheaper bronze coins,
"and as time went on was able to buy less and less."[20])

Seeing that altering the coinage did not halt the upward spiral of
prices, Diocletian tried a more direct approach. He decided that regu-
lating, or placing maximum caps on, prices and wages would stop
the rise of inflation and make goods and services affordable to more
people. He explained the theory behind his earnest but simple-minded
plan in the introduction to his famous economic edict, issued in 301.
We "hasten to apply the remedies long demanded by the [crippling
economic] situation," he said,

> satisfied that there can be no complaints. . . . With mankind it-
> self now appearing to be praying for release [from financial
> problems], we have decreed that there be established . . . a
> maximum [ceiling for prices and wages], so that when the
> violence of high prices appears anywhere—may the gods avert
> such a calamity! . . . It is our pleasure . . . that the prices listed

in the subjoined [attached] summary be observed in the whole
of our empire. [21]

Among the prices listed in the edict were 100 *denarii* for a bushel of
wheat, 30 for a bottle of quality aged wine, 12 for a pound of pork (the
Romans' favorite meat), and 16 for a pound of butter. Also, a carpen-
ter had to charge 50 *denarii* per day for his services, a baker 50, and a
sewer cleaner 25.

Even though Diocletian's edict had the force of law behind it,
this effort to cap prices failed. The exact reasons are not completely
clear, but it appears that many people resented being told what they
could earn or charge for goods. Whatever their motivations may have
been, a majority of citizens either ignored the new price caps or found
ways to get around them. One way was to trade one's own goods or
services in exchange for someone else's, eliminating the need for stan-
dardized money.

 Diocletian's Economic Edict

The following are excerpts from the opening section of Diocletian's edict of 301 (quoted in Lewis and Reinhold's *Roman Civilization,
Sourcebook II*), the purpose of which was to stabilize Rome's economy by setting maximum prices that people could charge for goods
and services.

> We, who by the gracious favor of the gods have repressed the
> former tide of ravages of barbarian nations by destroying them,
> must guard by the due defenses of justice a peace which was
> established for eternity. . . . It is the sole desire of unrestrained
> madness to have no thought for the common need. . . . [There-
> fore] we—the protectors of the human race . . . have agreed that
> justice should intervene . . . [and] apply the remedies long de-
> manded by the [crippling economic] situation. . . . With mankind
> itself now appearing to be praying for release [from economic
> misery], we have decreed that there be established . . . a maxi-
> mum [ceiling for prices and wages], so that when the violence
> of high prices appears anywhere—may the gods avert such a
> calamity! . . . It is our pleasure . . . that the prices listed in the sub-
> joined [attached] summary be observed in the whole of our em-
> pire. . . . [We] urge upon the loyalty of all our people that a law
> constituted for the public good may be observed with willing obe-
> dience and due care.

Taxes Paid in Kind

This sort of bartering system was nothing new for the inhabitants of the Empire. Because of the devaluation of coins and rampant inflation, Roman tax collectors had long accepted goods such as livestock, jewelry, and food as payment. In fact, by the early fourth century, payment in kind, then called *indictiones,* was the most common source of government tax revenue. The problem was that the tax collectors did not always gather the goods in a fair and equitable manner. Some rich people bribed them to get out of paying their fair share, and many poor people were unable to stop the collectors from taking everything of value. The state itself also suffered because revenue officials frequently had no idea how much would be collected in a given year and therefore could not effectively plan ahead.

To help alleviate these problems, Diocletian ordered a series of regional censuses. These surveys were designed to count the number of productive persons in the realm and determine the worth of their land, crops, livestock, and other property. The items were assessed in units of measure called *iuga.* According to Jones, each year government officials estimated

> how much wheat, barley, wine, meat, and [olive] oil were required to feed the army and the civil service and the population of [the city of] Rome [who by custom received free handouts of food] . . . and then [divided] the numbers by the number of *iuga.* . . . It only remained for the . . . [tax] collectors to extract the due amounts from the taxpayers."

Under Diocletian's immediate successors, including Constantine, this method of assessing people's worth and what they had to pay in *indictiones* remained in effect. In addition, there was at least some effort to make the system more equitable. For instance, a law passed during Constantine's reign stated that the "mass of the lower classes" should not "be subjected to the wantonness . . . of the more powerful and thus suffer the infliction of grave and iniquitous outrages."[23]

Such laws were not always enforced, however. Also, the government felt obliged to ensure that the number of productive taxpayers in various professions and social classes would remain more or less fixed. That way, the reasoning went, the government would encounter fewer shortfalls. To this end, Diocletian and his successors ordered that nearly all workers remain in their present professions for life. The sons of soldiers, ship captains, bakers, potters, weavers, miners, town councilors, and many others were expected to follow in their fathers' footsteps, whether they wanted to or not. This discouraged diversification, creativity, and progress, which ultimately had a stifling effect on the economy and produced a more regimented, despondent populace.

A Labor-Intensive System

Progress was also impeded by the primitive state of the economic system itself. Although Rome was one of the wealthiest and most advanced civilizations of the ancient world, its methods of production were quite backward by modern economic and technological standards. Except for a few brief periods when conditions were exceptionally good, more hungry mouths existed than the Empire's fields and gardens could feed. Farmers did rotate crops, allowing one field to lie vacant and replenish its nutrients while planting in another, but they often did not wait long enough and large areas suffered from soil depletion. Also, people spun yarn by hand and made cloth on clumsy hand looms. These and other methods of production were slow and relied too heavily on simple human and animal labor.

This labor-intensive system came under an immense strain in the late fourth century when the government had to pay and equip increasing numbers of soldiers to meet the threats posed by invading barbarians. To get the money and materials they needed, Roman officials raised taxes on a populace already exhausted by heavy taxation and efforts to make ends meet. This, along with other factors, led to a decline in the number of peasants, who had long occupied the sturdy base of the economic pyramid. "With primitive methods of agriculture, industrial production and transport," Jones explains,

> it took very many more man-hours than today to produce food. . . . Taxation had to be enormously increased, and to assess and collect the increased taxes, the civil service had to be expanded, thus increasing the taxation load again. The heavy burden of taxation was probably the root cause of the economic

As this engraving of Roman farm workers shows, technology was primitive and growing food was very labor intensive.

decline of the Empire. Marginal lands, which could not yield
a profit to the landlord over and above the taxes, ceased to be
cultivated. The population seems also to have shrunk. . . . There
are distinct signs of a chronic shortage of agricultural manpower, notably the reluctance of landlords to surrender their
tenants [dependent *coloni*] as recruits [for the army]. . . . The
peasantry, after paying their taxes, and the tenants their rent,
did not retain enough food to rear large families, and many
died of malnutrition or of actual starvation in bad seasons or
after enemy devastations. [24]

For these reasons, Rome's economy continued to undergo a slow
but steady decline. And when the days of reckoning came and the
realm sorely needed a strong, economically prosperous, resilient, and
hopeful populace to resist the onrush of the barbarians, none could be
found.

Increasing Political and Social Disunity

Chapter 3

B esides the Empire's steadily weakening economic conditions, other factors contributed to Rome's internal deterioration in the years preceding and during the major barbarian invasions of the fourth and fifth centuries. Some of these factors can be collectively called disunities or disharmonies. There was the Empire's political and geographical division into two distinct parts, for instance. Over the course of more than a century and a half, two increasingly separate Roman realms evolved. And when western Rome needed all the manpower, money, and other resources it could find to meet the challenge of the barbarian threat, it could no longer count on eastern Rome for much concrete aid.

Other disunities pitted one portion of, or group in, society against another. The rich often mercilessly exploited the poor, for example. And both the poor and the rich frequently resented the government and increasingly tried to escape its legal control. Meanwhile, rather than trying to Romanize the Germans who settled in Roman lands in the Later Empire, most people from traditional Roman families viewed them as racial and social inferiors. Treated as outsiders, these Germans often retained their own separate cultures. Instead of assimilating into Roman society, becoming loyal to Rome, and defending its ideals, they remained ethnically and often socially separate from the Roman mainstream. And this disunity, combined with the others, inevitably weakened the realm. Michael Grant sums it up this way:

> Italy and the entire Western world were hopelessly disunited.
> Rome did not fall only because of attacks from outside. . . .

Had they been the only trouble, the Empire might still have survived. . . . But by this time, it had become paralyzed by its internal disunities. . . . Each one of them was damaging. In accumulation, they proved fatal. By making resistance to the external onslaughts impossible, they swept the western Roman Empire out of existence.[25]

Dividing the Empire

Perhaps the most obvious disunity of the Later Empire was its political and physical division into two separate realms—one in the West, the other in the East. This separation, which ultimately fatally weakened western Rome, was a very gradual process. And that is why most people did not realize the danger it posed to the security of the West until it was too late.

As early as the second century, it became clear to some Roman leaders that the Empire was too huge for one ruler to administer either easily or well. Accordingly, Marcus Aurelius, last of the so-called good emperors, chose a co-ruler named Lucius Verus. When the barbarian invasions began during their reign, the attacks came in both West and East. While Aurelius took charge of the defenses in the West, he sent Verus to prosecute military operations in the East. Later, during

the last years of the Anarchy, the brothers Carinus and Numerian, who ruled the Empire jointly, divided military operations into western and eastern branches in a similar manner.

Carinus's and Numerian's immediate successor, Diocletian, carried this process a step further in the reforms that created the Later Empire. Diocletian believed that military affairs were not the only aspect of government that needed to be handled by two rulers. He also divided the regular administrative apparatus into western and eastern branches and himself took charge of the East, ruling from the city of Nicomedia (in northern Asia Minor). To rule the western sector, Diocletian selected a general named Maximian. (In 293, Diocletian further divided imperial power. He and Maximian each retained the title of Augustus and appointed an assistant emperor with the title of Caesar, creating a four-man ruling combination often referred to as the Tetrarchy.)

At this point, Rome's western and eastern portions were far from being separate empires. Diocletian was the senior ruler and therefore behind the scenes he had charge of the entire realm. Also, the West long remained the main center of power and prestige, partly because Italy was the traditional Roman heartland and Rome was viewed as the capital of the known world.

This perception began to change, however, when a later emperor, Constantine, built a splendid new eastern capital—Constantinople (the "city of Constantine"), which he dedicated in 330. His principal motivation was to establish a strong base from which to defend the Empire's eastern sphere against attacks from the north and east. The city's location, on the Bosporus Strait (the site of the Greek town of Byzantium), was a strategically strong position for the command and defense of Greece, Asia Minor, and the Black and Aegean seas. Moreover, Constantinople was intended from the beginning to be not simply an eastern supplement to Rome but, rather, its eastern equal. As Edward Gibbon wrote:

> The Imperial city commanded, from her seven hills, the opposite shore of Europe and Asia; the climate was healthy and temperate, the soil fertile, the harbor secure and [broad]; and the approach on the side of the continent [i.e., Europe] was of small extent and easy defense. . . . A multitude of laborers

A seventeenth-century painting depicts the emperor Constantine inaugurating the eastern capital of Constantinople.

... urged the conclusion of the work with incessant toil. ...
The buildings of the new city were ... decorated by the hands
of the most celebrated masters [of architecture, sculpture, and
painting]. ... By [Constantine's] commands, the cities of
Greece and Asia were despoiled of their most valuable orna-
ments [and brought to Constantinople]. ... The most fin-
ished statues of the gods and heroes, of the sages and poets
of ancient times, contributed to the splendid triumph of Constantinople. [26]

More important than Constantinople's buildings and statues was the
fact that it featured a full-fledged imperial court, where Constantine
held audience when he was in the East. He was sole ruler of the Empire for the second half of his reign. So the western and eastern courts
were still technically united in him.

Negative Long-Term Consequences

The next step in the evolution of the divided Roman Empire was for the western and eastern courts to each be ruled by a separate individual. This occurred most conspicuously under the emperors Valentinian I and Valens. After the troops hailed Valentinian emperor in 364, they expressed their desire that he nominate a second, backup emperor. That way, if he died unexpectedly, the succession would be assured and the transition to new leadership would go smoothly. (The former emperor, Jovian, had died without an heir and the army generals had been forced to conduct an extensive search for a suitable replacement.) In his inaugural address to the troops, Valentinian agreed to appoint a co-ruler. According to Ammianus, he told them, "I shall use my best efforts and fortune . . . [and make] a careful search [for] a man of steady character." Then Valentinian journeyed to Nicomedia,

> and on March 1 appointed his brother Valens . . . Augustus [emperor]. He dressed Valens in the imperial robes, placed a diadem [crown] on his head, and, sharing the same carriage, took him back to the city as his legitimate partner in power.[27]

Valentinian Addresses His Troops

As reported by Ammianus Marcellinus in his history of Rome, the following is part of the speech given to the soldiers by the newly enthroned emperor Valentinian I, one of the leading figures in the division of the Roman realm into two parts.

> Gallant defenders of our provinces, it is and will always be my pride and boast that I owe to your courage the rule of the Roman world, a position which I neither desired nor sought, but for which you have judged me to be the best qualified. . . . Now I must ask you to listen to me quietly while I explain in simple words what I think the welfare of the state requires. I do not doubt nor dispute that there are cogent reasons for the co-option of a colleague with equal status [i.e., a co-emperor] to meet all contingencies. I am only human, and I dread the accumulated responsibilities and various uncertainties that await me. But above all, we must strive for harmony, which brings strength out of weakness, and we shall easily attain it if you will be patient and fair-minded, and allow me the free exercise of my proper power.

The negative long-term consequences of Valentinian's appoint-
ment of his brother were not widely appreciated at the time. Valens
turned out to be more than a mere backup man for Valentinian. Given
full charge of the East, Valens sat on his own throne in Constantinople, and the two men divided up the army commanders and court officials. So there were now two distinct imperial courts, each oversee-
ing its own geographical sphere. However, Valentinian retained a sort
of seniority, as Diocletian had, and could overrule his brother if he
chose to; also, major policy for the Empire as a whole was still coor-
dinated by both rulers. Therefore, in reality there was still only a single Roman realm. To maintain the continuity of that realm and its leadership, in 367 Valentinian named his eight-year-old son Gratian as
co-emperor of the West. This proved a wise move. When Valentinian
died in 375, Gratian ascended the western throne and maintained close
relations with his uncle, Valens, in the East.

The final step in the gradual division of the Empire occurred on
the death of Theodosius I. Gratian had elevated him to the eastern throne
in 379 to replace Valens, who died fighting the Visigoths in the battle
of Adrianople. Later, after the deaths of Gratian and his half-brother
(Valentinian II), Theodosius ruled both the eastern and western Roman spheres from 394 to 395. He was the last emperor to do so.

When Theodosius died in 395, his two sons followed the succession plan he had arranged for them. Eleven-year-old Honorius took the
western throne, and seventeen-year-old Arcadius the eastern one. From
then on, the administrations and national policies of the two Roman
spheres were separate enough to produce what was seen as a *partes
imperii,* or "imperial realm made up of two distinct parts." Given that
the resources of the former single realm now had to be shared, each
part was inevitably militarily weaker and financially less well off
than the original Empire.

It was the West that ultimately suffered most from this division
of the Empire, however. In the short run the East survived, while the
West became weaker and more vulnerable to outside threats and finally disintegrated. A.H.M. Jones gives this insightful analysis of why
the eastern part of the realm outlasted the western part:

> In the first place, the western provinces were much more ex-
> posed to barbarian attack. The western emperor had to guard

Theodosius I, depicted on his throne, was the last emperor to rule both the western and eastern sections of the Empire.

the long fronts of the Rhine and the upper Danube, the eastern emperor only the lower Danube. . . . Moreover, if the western emperor failed to hold any part of the Rhine and Danube fronts, he had no second line of defense; the invaders could penetrate straight into Italy and Gaul, and even into Spain. The eastern emperor, if he failed, as he often did, to hold the lower Danube, only lost control temporarily of the [Danubian provinces]; for no enemy could force the Bosporus and the Hellespont, guarded by Constantinople itself. Asia Minor, Syria, and Egypt thus remained sealed off from invasion. . . . In the second place, the eastern parts [of the Empire] were . . . more populous, more intensely cultivated, and richer than the western. . . . [Also, the East] enjoyed much greater political stability and fewer of its resources were wasted in civil wars.[28]

The Poor vs. the State

Jones's point that the eastern part of the realm was richer than the West is telling. One way that the East was financially better off was in the area of taxation. Whereas most of the farms in the West were large tracts owned by wealthy landlords, a higher proportion of eastern farms were smaller and still owned by poor or middle-class farmers. These lower-class farmers did not have to give part of their harvests to rich overlords, so they kept more of what they produced. Also, most of the officials who managed the administration of the eastern provinces came from the middle classes (as opposed to the upper classes, as in the West). The personal fees these eastern administrators charged to collect the taxes were fairly reasonable, so taxes were generally lower in the East than in the West (where administrators added their higher fees to the already high tax burden on the poor).

The unfair, even brutal taxation of the lower classes in the western sector of the Later Empire did more than hurt the economy by devastating the agricultural base the realm sorely needed to sustain itself. Excessive taxation also turned large numbers of Romans against the government, creating a fatal disunity. The depth of the resentment the poor felt toward the state must have been great, for many poor farmers and laborers actually fled their homes to escape the tax collectors. Some even settled in areas taken over by barbarians, where Roman tax collectors could not reach them. The priest-writer Salvian described the sufferings of poor rural Romans in Gaul in the early to mid-fifth century in this eye-opening tract:

> What else can these wretched people wish for, they who suffer the incessant and even continuous destruction of public tax levies? To them there is always imminent a heavy and relentless proscription [government effort to find and ex-

ploit them]. They desert their homes, lest they be tortured in their very homes. They seek exile, lest they suffer torture. The enemy [i.e., the barbarians] is more lenient to them than the tax collectors. This is proved by the very fact that they flee to the enemy in order to avoid the full force of the heavy tax levy. . . . In the districts taken over by the barbarians, there is one desire among all the Romans, that they should never again find it necessary to pass under Roman jurisdiction [legal control]. In those regions, it is the one and general prayer of the Roman people that they be allowed to carry on the life they lead with the barbarians. And we wonder why the Goths are not conquered by our portion of the population, when the Romans prefer to live among them rather than with us.[29]

Thus, the government oppressed the peasants in one generation after another, which caused growing resentment among the lower classes. Therein lies a key factor in the realm's overall decline—a severe deterioration of morale, trust, and loyalty among the Romans themselves. The underprivileged "often found themselves driven into total destitution," Grant explains.

The People Stagger Beneath Their Debts

This anonymous fourth-century writing (quoted from Lewis and Reinhold's *Roman Civilization, Sourcebook II*), which thanks the emperor for helping a local community, captures some of the financial distress and agricultural devastation of the times.

I have told, O Emperor, how much the Aeduans deserved the aid you brought them; it follows that I should tell how serious was their distress. . . . Our community lay prostrate . . . from exhaustion of resources, ever since the severity of the new tax assessment had drained our very life. . . . Indeed, a field which never meets expenses is of necessity deserted; likewise the poor country folk, staggering beneath debts, were not permitted to bring in water or cut down forests, so that whatever usable soil there was has been ruined by swamps and choked with briers . . . everything waste, uncultivated, neglected, silent, shadowy—even military roads so broken . . . that scarcely half-filled, sometimes empty wagons cross them.

Between these rustic poor and the government, the relationship was that of oppressed and oppressor, of foe and foe. This
is perhaps the greatest of all the disunities that afflicted the
western Empire. The state and the underprivileged bulk of
its rural subjects were set against each other in a destructive
and suicidal disharmony, which played a very large and direct
part in the downfall that followed. It was because of this rift
[between the state and the poor] that the taxes which were
needed to pay for the army could not be raised. And because
they could not be raised, the Empire failed to find defenders,
and collapsed. [30]

The Rich vs. the State

Meanwhile, the poor were not the only group to lose confidence in and
distance itself from the government. Many members of the upper class

*This drawing illustrates the privileged, comfortable, carefree life enjoyed
by members of Rome's wealthy upper classes.*

increasingly came to feel that the emperor no longer supported their interests. There was a certain measure of jealousy and indignation involved because in the Later Empire the government often passed over wealthy landowners and promoted commoners to high administrative offices. The rich clearly felt a sense of entitlement, seeing themselves as better than those who were less well off. As one wealthy nobleman remarked in a letter that has survived, "good blood tells and never fails to recognize itself."[31] Such characters were often haughty and showed off their wealth in public whenever possible, as related in this passage from Ammianus's history:

> [They] think that the height of glory is to be found in unusually high carriages and an ostentatious [gaudy] style of dress; they sweat under the burden of cloaks which they attach to their necks and fasten at the throat. . . . They *contrive* by frequent movements . . . to show off their long fringes and display the garments beneath. . . . Others again, with an appearance of deep gravity, hold forth [speak] unasked on the immense extent of their family property, multiplying in imagination the annual produce of their fertile lands, which extend, they boastfully declare, from farthest east to farthest west. They presumably do not know that their ancestors, who were responsible for the expansion of Rome, did not owe their distinction to riches, but overcame all obstacles by their valor . . . Some [of the more arrogant rich], regardless of the risk, gallop their horses . . . through open spaces and paved streets of the city. . . . Behind them come their slaves in crowds like a gang of highwaymen [robbers] . . . [then come several armed guards, followed by] the stewards of a city household, whose rank is marked by a wand in their right hand. . . . Then comes the smoke-begrimed kitchen staff; after them the rest of the slaves . . . together with the idle populace of the neighborhood.[32]

Some of these idle rich showed off their wealth in ways that benefited the community; for instance by staging expensive public games. Yet as time went on, the government, which bore the primary responsibility for financing the games, grew more and more strapped for cash. And the state increasingly came to expect, and finally legally forced, the richest members of society to spend huge sums on the games. These people felt that they were getting little in return for such generosity, and their resentment for the government grew.

Their Own Petty Kingdoms

In addition, as the Empire's economy steadily deteriorated in the fourth and fifth centuries, most cities and towns declined and fell into disrepair. For centuries, most of the rich landowners had been urban-dwelling absentee landlords. No longer finding the cities worthwhile places to live, in the fourth century they began to withdraw to their country estates. There, "they might defy the tax collector, harbor refugees from justice, and in general comport themselves as little lords," writes classical scholar Harold Mattingly. "The central government was beginning to lose its grip, and something like the elements of a feudal system began to appear."[33]

These unusually large country estates featured gigantic, incredibly luxurious villas that were nothing short of palaces. They were also fortified like the palaces of the emperors to keep out not only marauding bands of barbarians but also government agents. Surrounded by dependent villages and farms, these estates "were whole little kingdoms unto themselves," says Grant, "self-contained economic and social units full of farm-workers, slaves, artisans, guards, bailiffs, and hangers-on." The rolling countryside of Gaul eventually had a major concentration of these petty kingdoms owned by a "vigorous aristocracy of about a hundred families." They "handed down their hereditary power" to their children and kept their own garrisons of armed troops.

> In 455, [at a] meeting at Arelate (Arles), they even proclaimed
> one of their own number, Avitus, as emperor. This act was a
> triumph of the Gallic nobles over the Roman aristocracy . . .
> though only a momentary one, since Avitus was deposed and
> died very soon afterwards. His son, Ecdicius, however, was
> still wealthy enough to support 4,000 starving poor in time
> of famine—a charity which by no means all his fellow
> landowners would have performed.[34]

This series of events shows clearly that in the fifth century, with the western Empire shrinking rapidly and a series of weak emperors

A Barbarian Noble and His Attendants

The Roman poet Sidonius lived among the barbarians in Gaul in the fifth century. In this excerpt from one of his surviving letters (translated by O.M. Dalton), he describes a German nobleman and his entourage.

> You [should] have seen the young prince Sigismer on the way to the palace of his father-in-law in the guise of a bridegroom . . . in all the pomp and bravery of the tribal fashion. . . . With charming modesty he went afoot amid his bodyguard and footmen, in flame-red mantle [cloak], with much glint of ruddy gold, and gleam of snowy silken tunic, his fair hair, red cheeks and white skin according with the three hues of his equipment. But the chiefs and allies who bore him company were dread of aspect. . . . Their feet were laced in boots of bristly [animal] hide reaching to the heels; ankles and legs were exposed. They wore high tight tunics. . . . Green mantles they had with crimson borders. . . . In their hands they grasped barbed spears and missile axes; their left sides were guarded by shields.

exercising less and less control, some rich people chose to distance themselves completely from the central government. Moreover, these country barons were not above dealing directly with the barbarians who had become their neighbors. And when the government in Ravenna fell in 476, these landed nobles saw further opportunity to maintain their wealth and influence. Some established close relations with Odoacer, the German general who deposed the last western emperor. In this way, part of the old Roman aristocracy survived the fall and transformed itself into a thriving part of the nobility of the Germanic kingdoms that supplanted the western Empire. Thus, fatal disunities among the Roman ranks hammered the final nails into the coffin in which the barbarian invasions had placed the last, pathetic vestiges of western Rome.

Christianity Weakens the Roman Spirit

Chapter 4

Edward Gibbon was the first modern historian to suggest that the rise and eventual triumph of Christianity in the Roman Empire was a major factor in the fall of that realm. In his view, one supported by most later scholars, the Christian faith weakened the traditional Roman state and society in a number of ways. First, during the Roman Empire the Christians were divisive because they would not tolerate other religions and condemned those who adhered to such faiths. Also, Christian leaders encouraged and sanctioned the idea of people dropping out of society to become solitary monks; this robbed the Empire of many of its most talented and creative members who might have helped the state solve its mounting problems.

Finally, and most importantly, Gibbon said, Christian beliefs were too pacifistic in the dangerous world in which Rome then existed. Christian leaders discouraged people from becoming public officials and especially soldiers. And by dampening Rome's old and venerable martial spirit, Christianity made the Empire more vulnerable to the foreign foes who threatened it, especially the northern barbarians. The Christians, Gibbon wrote, were

> offended by the use of oaths, by the pomp of magistracy [high public office], and by the active contention of public life, nor could their humane ignorance be convinced that it was lawful on any occasion to shed the blood of . . . fellow-creatures, either by the sword of justice, or by that of war, even [when hostile forces] should threaten the peace and safety of the whole community. . . . They refused to take any active part in the civil

administration or the military defense of the Empire. . . . It was impossible that the Christians . . . could assume the character of soldiers. . . . This . . . criminal disregard to the public welfare exposed them to the contempt and reproaches of the pagans [non-Christians], who very frequently asked, what must be the fate of the Empire, attacked on every side by the barbarians, if all mankind should adopt the [cowardly] sentiments of the new sect?[35]

The Anti-Christian Persecutions

The first anti-Christian persecution occurred under the emperor Nero (who reigned from 54 to 68). He accused the Christians of setting fire to Rome. "During his reign," wrote the second-century Roman historian Suetonius in his *Lives of the Twelve Caesars.* "a great many public abuses were suppressed by the imposition of heavy penalties. . . . Punishments were also inflicted on the Christians, a sect professing a new and mischievous religious belief." Other, larger-scale persecutions followed over the course of the centuries, including a particularly destructive one launched by the soldier-emperor Decius in 250. The worst of all was instigated in 303 largely by the eastern emperor Galerius, an avid Christian hater. The government ordered the closing of all Christian churches, the surrender and burning of holy books, and the banning of Christian religious meetings. Fortunately for the victims, only a decade later they gained toleration under Constantine.

Nero and his courtiers watch as several Christians are tied to posts (at right). They soon became human torches.

It is important to emphasize that Gibbon was not anti-Christian. In fact, he was a devout Christian himself. And in his masterwork he went on to praise the way Christianity softened the hard and cruel ways of many of the barbarians after they overran the western Roman realm. Gibbon and subsequent scholars examined the effects of Christian beliefs on Rome in a dispassionate manner, without making value judgments about either the Christian or pagan faiths. Instead, they tried to view the situation from the standpoint of average Romans in the fourth and fifth centuries. In that context, Christian beliefs and values, however inherently benevolent they may have been, were simply inconsistent with most traditional Roman beliefs and institutions. And the friction and rivalry between the two belief systems gradually weakened the older one, leaving the realm more vulnerable to attack by foreign enemies.

Christian Religious Exclusivity

The first pagan Roman charge against the Christians—that they were intolerant and divisive—stemmed partly from the feeling of religious exclusivity that they inherited from the Jews. The early Christian faith had sprung from Judaism, the faith of the Jews, in Roman-controlled Palestine in the first century A.D. (The southern portion of Palestine was known as Judaea, an area that had once been the site of the ancient Jewish kingdom of Judah. In A.D. 6, Judaea became an official province of the Roman Empire.) The Roman occupation of Palestine created considerable social disruption, insecurity, and despair among the locals, and helped to promote the spread of any beliefs that promised hope and salvation. A few Jewish preachers, Jesus and John the Baptist prominent among them, suggested that salvation might come sooner rather than later. They taught that the coming of the Messiah was imminent. This superhuman figure had long been prophesied in Jewish writings as one who would rescue the Jews from bondage and bring about God's kingdom on Earth.

Following Jesus' crucifixion by the Romans in about 30–33, his initial followers were Jews who believed that he had been the Messiah. Over time, however, the sect began to separate from Judaism proper, and by the end of the first century most of these followers called themselves Christians and non-Jews. Still, they recognized their Jewish

One of the many artistic depictions of Jesus' crucifixion. A generation later, his followers began to split with Judaism.

roots. For example, they viewed their single, all-powerful god as the same god of the Hebrew Old Testament. Also, the Christians retained the Old Testament as a sacred writing.

In addition, the monotheistic Jews had always seen themselves as set apart from other people, both spiritually and culturally. And the Christians inherited this feeling of special exclusivity, seeing the god of the Christians and Jews as the only god that existed. Most people in the Mediterranean world, however, viewed this position as religiously intolerant. Given this reality, it is not surprising that most other Romans long held the Jews and Christians in contempt. "The Jews refused to worship any god save their own, and declared all others to be false," A.H.M. Jones writes.

Jews were much disliked by their pagan neighbors, but [in a spirit of toleration] the Roman government steadily protected their cult and their right to follow their own religious law. . . . The other intolerant sect, which declared that the gods [worshiped by others] were . . . graven images or . . . demons, was Christianity. Christians were even more unpopular than the Jews. [36]

As Jones here mentions in passing, the main reason that most Romans saw the Jews and Christians as religiously intolerant was that pagan Romans were extremely tolerant regarding religion. This is evidenced by the Empire's broad proliferation of gods and beliefs. The Roman state promoted the sacred pantheon (group of gods), which included Jupiter (leader of the gods), his wife Juno (protector of women), and Mars (god of war). The Romans also welcomed a number of religions and gods from other lands, including Cybele from Asia Minor, Mithras from Persia, and Atargatis from Syria. Out of a sense of patriotism and shared tradition, people of all faiths paid at least occa-

The Edict of Toleration

The following is part of the Edict of Milan (quoted in Ehler and Morrall's *Church and State Through the Centuries*), issued in 313, which granted religious toleration to the Christians and restored their formerly confiscated property.

We, Constantine [ruler in the West] and Licinius [ruler in the East] . . . having met in concord in Milan . . . give both to Christians and to all others free facility to follow the religion which each may desire, so that by this means whatever divinity is enthroned in heaven may be gracious and favorable to us and to all who have been placed under our authority. . . . It is our pleasure that all restrictions which were previously put forward in official pronouncements concerning the sect of the Christians should be removed, and that each one of them who freely and sincerely carries out the purpose of observing the Christian religion may endeavor to practice its precepts without any fear or danger. . . . We have decided furthermore to decree the following in respect of the Christians: If those places at which they were accustomed in former times to hold their meetings . . . [have been confiscated by the state], let the [state] be willing and swift to restore them to the Christians.

sional homage to the state gods and also to the emperor, whom for political reasons the state represented as semidivine. In addition, members of one faith almost always showed respect for the gods of other
faiths. To most Romans, worshiping a certain god did not suggest
that all other gods were false or inferior. And most people matter-of-
factly accepted the notion that there were many diverse paths to the
same heavenly truths.

The Persecuted Become the Persecutors

Because the Christians rejected this notion of the equality and worth
of all gods and faiths, they stood out sharply and appeared to most people to be antisocial troublemakers. The Christians met and worshiped
in secret, which seemed suspicious; if they had nothing to hide, went
the common thinking, why not worship in the open like everyone else?
They also acquired the stigma of having *odium generis humani*, a "hatred for the human race." And because they refused to take part in
emperor worship and denied the existence of the state gods, Roman
officials came to see them as a potential threat to the safety of the realm.
As Jones puts it:

> It was commonly believed that [the Christians] practiced rit-
> ual infanticide [baby killing]—it no doubt leaked out that at
> their secret meetings they ate the flesh and blood of a son of
> man. . . . But the main charge against the Christians was that
> they were atheists, who denied and insulted all the gods. Or-
> dinary people naturally thought that the gods were angered by
> such impiety and might visit their wrath on the Empire which
> tolerated it. Whenever there was an earthquake or a famine the
> people called for the Christians to be thrown to the lions to ap-
> pease the angered gods. [37]

Throwing Christians into public arenas to be killed by wild beasts
was only one way that the Romans persecuted the Christians. The state
also ordered Christian meeting places and homes to be burned and destroyed sacred Christian writings. The rationale for the anti-Christian
persecutions, which occurred off and on for about three centuries, was
that the Christians were an antisocial, criminal element that needed
to be restrained and punished before they seriously harmed the community. The Christians bravely persevered, however, and survived

the persecutions. In the early fourth century, with the invaluable aid of the emperor Constantine I, who granted the Christians toleration (in 313, in the famous Edict of Milan), they began to gain a measure of respect and social acceptance.

Yet Roman society became increasingly polarized, mainly because distrust between pagans and Christians continued. This time, anti-Christian feelings were fueled by Christians turning the tables on the pagans. As the emperors converted to the faith and Christians gained more and more political power, pagans often found themselves the targets of religious intolerance and persecution. Urged on by Christian bishops, Michael Grant writes, the government eventually

> sought to enforce conformity upon all who did not agree with the doctrines of
> the official church. . . . This willingness to use forcible methods was based on a disastrous interpretation of the text in the Gospel according to St. Luke, in which Jesus was declared to have said, "go out into the highways . . . *and compel them to come in,* that my house may be filled." In the later Roman world, this sentence . . . was used by church and state as an invitation to the fatal policy of coercion.[38]

In the increasingly pro-Christian social and political climate, paganism came under attack. Some Christians vandalized or destroyed pagan statues, shrines, and temples across the realm, while zealous Christian priests denounced pagan beliefs and worship from the pulpit.

Ambrose Urges the Suppression of Paganism

The most influential of these bishops was Ambrose of Milan (born ca. 340), who helped to complete the Christian revolution that Constantine had started. Ambrose showed no tolerance or respect for the religious views of others. He felt that his own faith was the only true one and that pagan beliefs must be suppressed and eradicated. To this end, he per-

Christians become martyrs in a Roman arena. In the fourth century, they gained respectability and political power.

suaded the western emperor Gratian to relinquish his post as chief priest of the state religion, which all emperors since Augustus had held.

This effectively reduced the spiritual authority of the emperors, who were thereafter expected to recognize the authority of the Christian bishops in religious affairs. Over time, this contributed to a partial surrender of imperial power to the clergy. "The distinction of the spiritual and temporal [worldly] powers, which had never been imposed on [Rome's] free spirit," Gibbon wrote,

> was introduced and confirmed by the legal establishment of Christianity. . . . In the Christian Church, which entrusts the service of the altar to . . . consecrated ministers, the monarch . . . was seated below the rails of the sanctuary, and confounded [placed on the same level] with the rest of the faithful multitude. The emperor might be saluted as the father of his people, but he owed a filial duty and reverence to the fathers of the Church. [39]

Ambrose vs. Symmachus

The confrontation between the bishop Ambrose and pagan noble-man Symmachus over the restoration of the statue of the goddess Victory was a bitter one. Addressing the emperor, Symmachus pleaded (as quoted in volume 10 of *A Select Library of Nicene and Post-Nicene Fathers,* Series II):

> We demand . . . the restoration of that condition of religious affairs which was so long advantageous to the state. . . . We beseech you . . . for peace for the gods of our fathers and of our country. It is just that all worship should be considered as one. We look on the same stars, the sky is common [to all], the same world surrounds us. What difference does it make by what pains each seeks the truth? We cannot attain to so great a secret by one road.

Ambrose responded:

> [Symmachus,] your sacrifice is a rite of being sprinkled with the blood of beasts. Why do you seek the voice of God in dead animals? . . . By one road, says he, one cannot attain to so great a secret. What you know not . . . we know by the voice of God. . . . Your ways, therefore, do not agree with ours. . . . You worship the works of your own hands; we think it an offense that anything which can be made should be esteemed God. God wills not that He should be worshipped in stones.

Ambrose also convinced Gratian to take away government funding for the state priesthood and to remove the time-honored statue of the goddess Victory from the Roman Senate. Viewing the latter act as both intolerant and insensitive, leading pagans called on a respected senator, Quintus Symmachus, to plead their case to the state. Ambrose's influence was too strong, however, and the statue was never returned to the Senate.

Now the most powerful religious figure in the Roman world, Ambrose struck further blows against paganism, in the process stirring up more hatred and divisions between pagans and Christians. The crusading bishop exerted a strong influence on Gratian's successor, Theodosius I, whom Ambrose at first deemed too respectful of non-Christians. In one celebrated incident, some militant Christians burned down a Jewish synagogue. Part of the penalty meted out by Theodosius was for the arsonists to rebuild the structure. But Ambrose told the emperor that it would be improper to force Christians to construct a Jewish place of worship. Theodosius gave in, the synagogue was never rebuilt, and the arsonists were never punished. In the words of noted Christian scholar Justo Gonzalez, "This was a sad precedent, for it meant that in an empire calling itself Christian, those whose faith was different would not be protected by the law."[40]

Later, Theodosius agreed to other important demands made by Ambrose and other powerful bishops. In the early 390s, the emperor prohibited all pagan sacrifices and cults and closed the pagan temples. (Some were destroyed, others converted into museums, and still others remodeled as Christian churches.) Soon the Olympic Games (which were dedicated to the Greek god Zeus, equivalent to the Roman Jupiter) were banned too, as were many other pagan religious festivals.

These acts fostered heightened hostility for Christianity among the pagans, who still constituted a majority of the population. Pagan wor-

This detail from a painting by the Renaissance Italian master Giotto shows the bishop Ambrose studying the Scriptures.

ship defiantly continued in private settings. And more and more pagans came to believe that the recent barbarian attacks were actually the fault of the Christians. These invasions, along with Rome's sacking in 410, were widely seen as punishments sent by the traditional Roman gods for Christianity's denial and mistreatment of them. In response, the renowned Christian leader Augustine wrote *The City of God,* which claimed the opposite was true—namely, that the pagans' sins and denial of the Christian god had brought about these disasters.

These strong religious differences and resentments remained in effect throughout the fifth century. And they divided and embittered the Roman population to such a degree that they were unable to present a united front against the onrushing tide of barbarians. The damage done by the Christians' refusal to respect and accept other beliefs was major, says Grant, "and Gibbon was right to blame the hostility between . . . Christian and pagan for helping to bring down the Empire."[41]

The Religious Dropouts

Christianity delivered another blow to the traditional stability of Roman society by encouraging people to leave their regular lives and become monks, nuns, and other religious recluses. This was the monastic movement (from the Greek word *monachos,* meaning "solitary"). Although the movement eventually spread throughout the Empire, at first it was most popular in the East, especially in the remote reaches of the Egyptian deserts.

At least in part, the monastic movement was a reaction to the faith's new, more comfortable place in society. Some of the more devout Christians worried that the church might become too worldly and its leaders too comfortable. As Gonzalez points out, a number of people converted to the faith to enhance their social status and position.

> Bishops competed with each other after prestigious positions. The rich and powerful seemed to dominate the life of the Church. . . . How was one to be a true Christian in such circumstances? . . . How to overcome Satan, who is constantly tempting the faithful with the new honors that society offers? Many found an answer in the monastic life—to flee from human society, to leave everything behind, to dominate the body

This illustration from a thirteenth-century Spanish manuscript shows scenes from the secluded and strict monastic life.

and its passions, which gave way to temptation. Thus, at the very time when churches in large cities were flooded by thousands demanding baptism, there was a veritable exodus of other thousands who sought beatitude [blessedness] in solitude. [42]

Many bishops were initially troubled by the monastic movement. This was partly because those who were leaving the Christian communities were among their most dedicated and thoughtful members. In time, though, leading clergymen came to accept and praise the movement. For example, Athanasius, who became bishop of Alexandria, Egypt, in 328, wrote an approving biography of Anthony, a well-known monk. The work became very popular and inspired thousands of Christians to join the monastic movement.

For the Christian Church, the monastic movement was a profound expression of love for and duty to God. For the traditional Roman Empire, by contrast, it was a weakening force that encouraged a debilitating drain on society's precious human resources. From the viewpoint of Roman non-Christians, the converts abandoned their normal

An eighteenth-century engraving portrays Athanasius, whose biography of the monk Anthony became widely popular.

responsibilities to community and country. This was seen as especially bad after the major barbarian attacks began in the late 370s. As Grant puts it, the monastic dropouts

> often shook the dust of the social, financial, and political system off their feet as completely as if they had never belonged to it at all. And so, as the final political and military reckoning [of the fifth century] rapidly approached, this substantial number of men and women was no longer available to contribute either to the actual defense of the Empire or to the revenue needed to pay for the defenders. [43]

Soldiers of Christ?

Christianity also weakened Rome's defenses by working to suppress its traditional martial spirit, the ingrained belief in military strength and preparedness that had allowed it to build and successfully defend its mighty empire. "It might seem somewhat surprising," says Grant,

> that after the Empire became Christian, the Church and its leaders, although they were now partners of the emperor, still persisted in their old conviction that Christianity was incompatible with state service. Indeed, Christian leaders of the time . . . still continued to speak out frequently and openly against military service. [44]

Examples of this growing hostility toward military affairs abounded. The bishop Athanasius praised Christian pacifism, declaring that the only true enemy of Christians was evil itself. And Martin of Tours (born ca. 316), a pagan soldier who converted to Christianity and became an influential monk, publicly renounced his military service. "I have served you as a soldier," he is reported to have said.

> Allow me now to become a soldier to God. . . . I am the soldier of Christ, [so] it is not lawful for me to fight. If this conduct of mine is ascribed to cowardice, and not to faith, I will take my stand unarmed before the line of battle tomorrow, and in the name of the Lord Jesus, protected by the sign of the cross, and not by shield or helmet, I will safely penetrate the ranks of the enemy. [45]

According to the story, Martin did not have to prove himself in this manner, for the enemy soon surrendered.

Martin of Tours renounces his weapons. Martin believed that the Christian cross would better protect him and Rome.

That Martin refused to fight and kill was not unusual for a devout Christian of his day. More and more members of the faith took to heart the words of Basil, Bishop of Caesaria (on the coast of Palestine). He warned that any soldier who killed someone in the performance of his duty was guilty of murder and must be excommunicated from the church. A bishop named Paulinus echoed the same sentiment, saying:

> Do not any longer love this world or its military service, for
> Scripture's authority attests that whoever is a friend of this
> world is an enemy of God. He who is a soldier with the sword
> is the servant of death, and when he sheds his own blood or
> that of another, this is the reward for his service. [46]

Hearing such ideas preached in sermons, increasing numbers of young Roman men no longer aspired to soldiering. "The command to 'turn the other cheek', attributed to Jesus," Grant points out, "made it difficult for a Christian to be a Roman soldier . . . and there were numerous specific instances of men, who, after embracing Christianity, felt unable to serve in the army any longer." [47] Moreover, many of the native Romans who were forced into service and faced the barbarian assaults of the fifth century lacked the fighting spirit of their ancestors. Indeed, it was not unusual for such recruits to throw down their arms and run away at the moment when their country needed them most. Not surprisingly, when old-fashioned Roman patriotism died, the Empire was doomed.

Fatal Deterioration
of the Roman Army

conomic decline, division of the Empire, severe social disunities, and the social and psychological effects of Christianity
all played roles in weakening the Roman realm and making it
more vulnerable to the barbarian invasions. Each of these factors also
indirectly and negatively affected the Roman military. The fatal decline
of the once great Roman army had other causes as well. These included
major changes in military strategy, the incorporation of too many barbarian troops into the ranks, a breakdown in discipline, and the military's increasing loss of prestige. The deterioration of the army was un-
doubtedly second only to the barbarian invasions themselves as a primary cause for western Rome's decline and fall. Simply put, when the
last, degraded vestiges of the army could no longer effectively defend
the Empire, that realm could no longer survive.

Qualities of the Traditional Army

This dire outcome for the twelve-hundred-year-old Roman state became inevitable only in its last century or so. The traditional Roman
army that existed before the Later Empire was well up to the task of
fending off the barbarians. This is proven by the fact that Rome was
able to repel all of the earlier Germanic invasions (as well as attacks
by other peoples, such as the Celts and Persians).

Part of the Romans' long success in military affairs is attribut-
able to their traditional overall strategy. Military historians often re-
fer to it as "preclusive security." Essentially, it consisted of making the
borders as impenetrable as possible by stationing the bulk of the ac-

tive troops in permanent fortresses on or near the borders. Invaders only occasionally broke through these defenses. And when they did, the government was generally able to move in troops from other regions to thwart the intruders.

Another strength of the traditional Roman military was its heavy reliance on infantry (foot soldiers). Roman soldiers (called legionaries) were tough, well trained, and highly disciplined and fought in flexible, efficient formations. These formations ultimately broke down into a series of lines in such a way that while the men in one line attacked, others held back and waited for the order to enter the fray and relieve their comrades. Arther Ferrill, author of a major recent study on the Roman military, elaborates, saying that in the traditional army

> soldiers were not expected to fight to the death before being replaced by men from the rear. There was a regular rotation of fighting waves. . . . Although the efficient use of manpower in the Roman army was obviously important, the psychological advantages of such a system were enormous. Because . . . soldiers in the front of the line could expect to be reinforced in the course of fighting, they fought confidently, and knew in the depths of their souls that their comrades-in-arms to the rear would not leave them in the lurch. . . . Against untrained troops, they simply could not be defeated, even when they were greatly outnumbered.[48]

There were exceptions to this rule. But almost always Roman military defeats occurred when the Romans were surprised and surrounded, as in the disaster in the Teutoburg Forest in A.D. 9.

In contrast, the Germans and other barbarians usually employed less formidable and effective formations. Typically, they massed most of their warriors together in a large group, often in the shape of a square. Such a formation had depth, but it was disorganized and had little flexibility. Also, barbarian armies tended to engage most or all of their warriors at the same time, so when the fighters became exhausted (which happened in under an hour) they had no reserve force to back them up.

In addition, barbarian warriors often carried weapons that lacked the effectiveness of those wielded by traditional Roman legionaries. This difference proved crucial to the outcomes of many battles, including the battle fought at Mons Graupius in southern Scotland in

Traditional Roman Shields and Swords

In his *Histories,* the Greek historian Polybius gave this description of the shield and sword wielded by Roman legionaries in the late Republic and early Empire.

> The Roman panoply [array of armor and weapons] consists in the first place of a long shield (*scutum*). The surface is convex [curved]; it measures two and a half feet in width and four in length, and the thickness at the rim is a palm's breadth. It consists of two layers of wood fastened together with bull's hide glue; the outer surface is then covered first with canvas and then with calf-skin. The upper and lower edges are bound with iron to protect the shield both from the cutting strokes of swords and from wear. . . . Besides the shield, they also carry a sword [*gladius*], which is worn on the right thigh. . . . This has a sharp point and can deal an effective blow with either edge, as the blade is very strong and unbending.

The scutum *(shield),* gladius *(sword), and the* pilum *(throwing spear) are accurately depicted in this drawing.*

A typical barbarian soldier fought bare-chested, wore little or no armor, and wielded a broadsword and small shield.

A.D. 84. A Roman army led by Gnaeus Julius Agricola confronted a larger force of Caledonian (Scottish) barbarians. The Caledonians fought with small shields and large broadswords, while each Roman carried his longer, more protective rectangular shield (the *scutum*) and shorter, pointed thrusting sword (the *gladius*). According to Agricola's son-in-law, the great Roman historian Tacitus:

> At last Agricola [ordered several units of his best veterans] to close and fight it out at the sword's point. These old soldiers had been well-drilled in sword-fighting, while the enemy were awkward at it, with their small shields and unwieldy swords,

80 FALL OF THE ROMAN EMPIRE

especially as the latter, having no points, were quite unsuitable for a cut-and-thrust struggle at close quarters. The [Romans], raining blow after blow, striking them with the bosses of their shields, and stabbing them in the face, felled the [Caledonians in great numbers].[49]

A More In-Depth Strategy

The surviving ancient sources suggest that the Germans and other barbarians who attacked Rome in later centuries did not employ weapons and tactics significantly different from those of the Caledonians. The problem for Rome was that its own military did change over time. The great disparity in quality that originally existed between the average Roman army and the average barbarian one slowly diminished over the course of Rome's last centuries. Eventually, virtually no difference existed between the two.

The reasons for this momentous Roman military decline were many and varied. One of the most significant was related to an overall change in strategy on the part of the emperors and military generals. At the dawn of the Later Empire, Diocletian instituted a series of military reforms that his immediate successors, including Constantine, continued and elaborated on. Mainly defensive in nature, the new strategy moved away from the concept of preclusive security, in which most troops occupied static positions in the frontiers near the border areas. Essentially, it recognized a new and unpleasant reality— that during large-scale invasions some invaders should be expected to get through the line of forts along these frontiers.

However, Roman leaders reasoned, the attackers could still be stopped by a more layered, in-depth approach to defense. The idea was to station a few small, swiftly moving mobile armies at key points well inside the northern provinces. These mobile forces could hopefully intercept any enemy army that was able to cross through the frontiers. To make such "defense-in-depth" strategy work, Ferrill points out, the frontier forts had to be "strong enough to withstand attack and yet not so strongly defended as to become a drain on manpower weakening the mobile army."[50] Using this approach, Diocletian stationed small armies, each accompanied by detachments of cavalry, at various places in the northern provinces. If necessary, the cavalry units could leave their bases, fight the enemy,

A twelfth-century religious medallion shows Constantine's troops defeating an enemy force.

and then return to the bases. He also attached two highly trained units of legionaries to his personal traveling court. These were supported by an elite cavalry force, constituting a fast and very effective mobile field army.

Constantine's Military Reforms

Later, Constantine took these military reforms a step further. Like Diocletian, he divided his military into both mobile forces and frontier border guards. However, Constantine withdrew more troops from the frontier forts and used them to create several small mobile armies that were almost constantly on the move. These forces patrolled the northern provinces, traveling from town to town. At least in theory, that made it more difficult for an enemy army to know how close such a force was and from what direction it would strike.

It is important to point out that these individual field armies were tiny in comparison to traditional Roman armies of earlier eras. Each of Constantine's mobile army units probably numbered little more than a thousand infantry and five hundred cavalry. [51] These units were sometimes combined to form larger armies. But only rarely did generals in the Later Empire field forces numbering in the tens of thousands. (Thus, Valens's army of between fifty and sixty thousand at Adrianople was highly exceptional.) Whatever the strategies employed, the decreasing size of average Roman forces was symptomatic of the steady decline of the military in the Later Empire.

In fact, modern scholars are not alone in seeing the weaknesses of Rome's military reforms in that era. Zosimus, a fifth-century Greek historian, was convinced that Constantine's emphasis on small mobile

A modern reenactor displays the typical armor and weapons of a Roman infantryman of the late fourth century.

armies had left the frontiers too vulnerable to attack. In his *Historia Nova,* a chronicle of Roman history from Augustus's reign to his own time, Zosimus wrote:

> Constantine abolished this [frontier] security by removing the greater part of the soldiery from the frontiers to cities that

needed no auxiliary [extra supporting] forces. He thus deprived of help the people who were harassed by the barbarians [i.e., those who lived on or near the borders] and burdened tranquil cities with the pest of the military, so that several [of these cities] were straightaway deserted. Moreover, he softened the soldiers, who treated themselves to shows [public games] and luxuries [in the cities]. Indeed (to speak plainly) he personally planted the first seeds of our present devastated state of affairs.[52]

Another negative outcome of the new dependence on mobile armies was that over time it undermined and weakened the most effective branch of the traditional Roman army—the infantry. "Naturally in a mobile army the most mobile units, cavalry, will tend to be favored," Ferrill writes.

> With the emergence of cavalry and the decline of infantry . . . [especially] along the frontiers, Rome's military position went into a tailspin, for . . . the great battles of the coming decades were decided by infantry. Traditional Roman military tactics, [built around infantry and] driven by harsh discipline and constant training, simply disappeared. . . . Except for heavy cavalry . . . body armor was almost abandoned by the Roman army. While cavalry wore . . . metal helmets, infantry had only leather caps. By the end of the fourth century, weapons and weapons training had deteriorated drastically from earlier standards, undoubtedly because the new strategic role of the frontier troops gave them less significant responsibilities and did not demand as much of them tactically. The grand strategy of Constantine took a terrible toll in military efficiency.[53]

Barbarization of the Roman Ranks

Also damaging to military efficiency was a slow but steady breakdown in traditional Roman regimentation and discipline, which had long been renowned throughout the known world. This trend was caused mainly by a phenomenon that modern historians call the "barbarization" of the Roman army. The process began in prior centuries when the government had allowed Germans from beyond the northern borders to settle in Roman lands. Once these settlers had established themselves, they were more than willing to fight Rome's enemies, including fellow Germans. The Roman government came to see this as a boon. After the great Roman defeat at Adrianople in 378, Roman generals needed new soldiers more than ever, and Theodosius began to recruit Germans in much greater numbers than any leader before him. Indeed, his victory at the Frigidus River in the early 390s would not have been possible without the twenty thousand Visigoths he sent in human waves against his foes.

As the recruitment of barbarians into the army ranks accelerated, however, this policy began to affect the discipline of the troops and their willingness to fight and die for Rome. Both of these qualities diminished over time, until finally they nearly disappeared, since by the 440s almost all of the men in the army were Germans rather than native Romans. According to Ferrill, as early as the 380s the German recruits

> began immediately to demand great rewards for their service and to show an independence that in drill, discipline and organization meant catastrophe. They fought under their own native commanders, and the barbaric system of discipline was in no way as severe as the Roman. Eventually Roman soldiers saw no reason to do what barbarian troops in Roman service were rewarded heavily for not doing. . . . Too long and too close association with barbarian warriors, as allies in the Roman army, had ruined the qualities that made Roman armies great. . . . The Roman army of A.D. 440, in the West, had become little more than a barbarian army itself. . . . Fighting ability on the field, the drive to control that no-man's zone between two hostile armies facing one another in combat, was gone. . . . The stagnating effect of defeat and the disturbing influx of barbarian laxness in matters of drill and discipline destroyed the greatest fighting force the world had yet seen or would know again until the age of Napoleon.[54]

The military barbarization process in the western Empire's final century also contributed to significant changes in armor. Most Roman body armor in the Later Empire consisted of a linen or leather tunic covered with rows of thin bronze or iron rings (called mail) or scales. Such armor was by no means foolproof, but it protected the wearer well

A Late Roman Battlefield Formation

During the fourth and fifth centuries, Roman military units increasingly adopted German-style formations and tactics. Perhaps the most common late Roman battlefield formation was the *cuneus*, which modern scholars used to think was shaped like a wedge or arrowhead. The *cuneus* was more likely a square or rectangular attack column made up of a dense mass of men. Its width probably averaged twenty-five men and its depth sixteen men, though this likely varied from one place and time to another. "Once the men in the column launched a charge," historian Simon Macdowall suggests in his *Late Roman Infantrymen*, "the neat alignment of the ranks and files would naturally be lost and the men in the center, feeling more secure, would surge forward, while those to the flanks [sides] might hang back." For this reason, the formation could quickly become disorganized and lose its cohesion.

enough as long as he was not the victim of a direct, forceful thrust by a sword, spear, or arrow. Mail and scale armor were not cheap. And after the disaster at Adrianople, the government lacked the financial resources to supply all the troops with such protection. Over time, more and more soldiers had to purchase or borrow their own armor. Some wore whatever they could afford to scrape together, and increasing numbers wore no armor at all, especially in the fifth century. Another reason for this trend was that a larger percentage of the army ranks came to be filled by Germans, who frequently viewed such armor as uncomfortable and unnecessary. Vegetius, a late-fourth-century Roman civil servant who wrote a handbook on military matters, reported:

> We have made some improvements in the arms of the cavalry, [but] it is plain that the infantry are completely exposed. From the foundation of the city until the reign of the emperor Gratian [who died in 383], foot soldiers wore cuirasses [chest protectors] and helmets. But negligence and sloth having by degrees introduced a total relaxation of discipline, the soldiers began to consider their armor too heavy and seldom put it on. They first requested leave [asked] . . . to lay aside the cuirass and afterwards the helmet. [55]

Military barbarization also caused changes in weapons and battle tactics. Late Roman army weapons were an eclectic collection of

In Rome's last century, soldiers increasingly abandoned heavy armor and adopted several barbarian-style weapons.

items; some evolved from earlier Roman ones, but many had been popular among barbarian warriors. These included a long sword worn on the left side; a javelin (throwing spear); a bow; a throwing ax (introduced by the Franks and other Germans); and the *plumbata*, a lead-weighted dart about twenty inches long. (A soldier carried five darts on a small rack mounted on the inside of his wooden shield.) As for battle tactics, the infantry increasingly came to fight barbarian-style, in a poorly organized mass of troops.

Draft Dodgers and Deserters

In addition to factors associated with the barbarization of the army, the Roman military continued to decline for other reasons. As both the central government and local leaders encountered more and more economic problems, the tasks and duties of the average Roman soldier became more thankless and hopeless. The soldiers not only received little pay, but their wages were often months or even years overdue, which severely damaged morale. Serving in the military, once a prestigious and coveted goal, steadily lost its allure for native Romans. Recruiting new nonbarbarian soldiers therefore became more and more difficult.

The problem of recruiting native Romans became even worse in the last two decades of the fourth century and on into the fifth, especially in the western portion of the realm. This was partly because the western provinces were less populous than the eastern ones. The increasingly widespread refusal of Christians to join and fight was also a contributing factor. In response, the government became desperate and not only recruited more barbarians but also passed laws designed to force native Romans into the army.

Such laws only made matters worse. The effort to escape military service, either legally or illegally, became a major pastime at all levels of society. Michael Grant writes:

> Hosts of Senators, bureaucrats and clergymen were entitled to avoid the draft, and among other groups who escaped [legally] were cooks, bakers and slaves. To draw the rest of the population into the levy, the combing-out process was intensive. Even the men in the emperor's own very extensive estates found themselves called up. Yet other great landlords proved far less

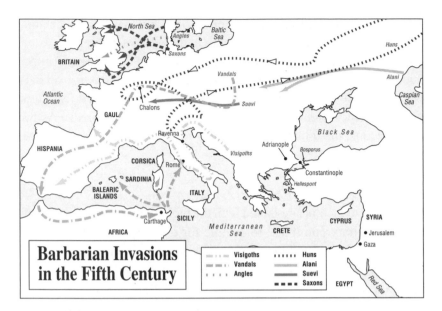

Barbarian Invasions in the Fifth Century

cooperative. They were supposed to furnish army recruits in proportion to the size of their lands. But on many occasions they resisted firmly.[56]

As more of the landed nobles hid potential army recruits to keep them for their own exploitation, the government cracked down. In 440 it made such concealment punishable by death. Yet this approach had little effect, since government agents feared risking their lives by entering and searching the great estates, which were crawling with armed men loyal to their local lords.

Meanwhile, some potential recruits resorted to extreme measures to dodge the draft, including cutting off their own thumbs. When this practice became widespread, the government at first ordered that such shirkers be burned alive. But later, as the authorities became more desperate, they let such self-mutilated individuals live and forced them to serve in the army despite their handicap. The state also ordered that new recruits have their skin branded with easily visible insignia, like runaway slaves did, so that they would be easier to track down if they deserted.

Rome's Fading Twilight

As these problems grew worse and took their toll over time, the traditional Roman soldier and army—highly disciplined, well organized and trained, tough and tenacious, eager and willing to defend both family and the Roman state—steadily deteriorated. Exactly how much this contributed to the fall of the western Empire cannot be measured precisely after the passage of so many centuries. After all, this was but one of many causes that combined to bring down that great realm. As scholars Pat Southern and Karen Dixon put it in their comprehensive survey of the Roman military's last centuries:

> A history of the late Roman army is inextricably [unavoidably] bound up with the fate of the Empire and the reasons why the western half fragmented and the eastern half survived into and beyond the early Byzantine era. Probably no single satisfactory explanation will ever be formulated to answer the question of why the Empire fell, nor even how, nor exactly when.[57]

Yet as modern historians devote more and more attention to the causes of western Rome's fall, the decline of the army looms ever larger and more conspicuous. The plain fact, say Southern and Dixon, is that

> the western Empire turned into the Frankish, Visigothic, and Ostrogothic kingdoms, and the Roman army disappeared. The East retained its army, but it was only partially recognizable

Rome's Swan Song

In this tract from the *Voyage Home to Gaul* (quoted in Duff and Duff's *Minor Latin Poets*), the poet Rutilius Namatianus delivered what modern historians have come to call "Rome's swan song."

> Listen, O fairest queen of your world, Rome, welcomed amid the starry skies, listen, you mother of men and mother of gods, thanks to your temples we are not far from heaven. . . . Sooner shall guilty oblivion overwhelm the sun than the honor due to you quit my heart. For your benefits extend as far as the sun's rays, where the circling Ocean-flood bounds the world. . . . For nations far apart you have made a single fatherland; under your dominion captivity has meant profit even for those who knew not justice: and by offering to the vanquished a share in your own justice, you have made a city of what was formerly a world. . . . Spread forth the laws that are to last throughout the ages of Rome. Alone you need not dread the . . . Fates. . . . The span [of Rome's reign] which remains is subject to no bounds, so long as earth shall stand firm and heaven uphold the stars!

as a Roman army. . . . Whatever the truth about the disap-
pearance of the army, the effect was most crucially felt by
the generations of people who witnessed the [destructive] transformation [of the army and the realm].[58]

Thus, the army's loss of effectiveness, combined with serious economic and other problems, was simply too much for the decaying
Roman system to bear. In the face of the continuing barbarian invasions, the western realm eroded, buckled, and eventually collapsed.
Even up to the bitter end, many Romans failed to recognize that their
traditional world was disintegrating around them. They simply could
not imagine a universe whose center was not occupied by Rome, much
as most Americans today cannot envision that their own nation is,
like all others in history, subject to the inevitable ravages of time,
change, and decay.

An example of such self-denial in Roman civilization's fading twi-
light has survived. Penned in about 416 by the Roman poet Rutilius
Namatianus, it expresses the earnest belief that the Empire will survive and regain its formal glory. The tract reads in part:

> Listen, O fairest queen of your world, Rome . . . you mother
> of men and mother of gods . . . sooner shall guilty oblivion
> overwhelm the sun than the honor due to you quit my heart.
> For your benefits extend as far as the sun's rays. . . . The span
> [of Rome's reign] which remains [in the future] is subject to
> no bounds, so long as Earth shall stand firm and heaven up-
> hold the stars![59]

Only sixty years after these words were written, the western Roman
Empire finally succumbed to total defeat and ceased to exist.

Notes

Introduction: The Giant Shadow of Rome's Fall

1. Chester G. Starr, *The Roman Empire, 27 B.C.–A.D. 476: A Study in Survival.* New York: Oxford University Press, 1982, p. 3.
2. Max Cary, "The Roman Empire: Retrospect and Prospect," in Mortimer Chambers, ed., *The Fall of the Roman Empire: Can It Be Explained?* New York. Holt, Rinehart, and Winston, 1963, p. 111.
3. André Piganiol, *L'Empire Chrétien.* Paris: University Presses of France, 1972, p. 466.
4. Edward Gibbon, *The Decline and Fall of the Roman Empire,* 1776–1788; reprint, ed. David Womersley, 3 vols. New York: Penguin, 1994, vol. 2, p. 511.
5. Arther Ferrill, *The Fall of the Roman Empire: The Military Explanation.* New York: Thames and Hudson, 1986, p. 22.

Chapter 1: Barbarians Overrun the Roman Realm

6. Gibbon, *Decline and Fall,* vol. 2, p. 512.
7. Suetonius, *Augustus,* in *Lives of the Twelve Caesars,* published as *The Twelve Caesars,* trans. Robert Graves, rev. Michael Grant. New York: Penguin, 1979, p. 65.
8. Michael Grant, *The Fall of the Roman Empire.* New York: Macmillan, 1990, p. 3.
9. Ammianus Marcellinus, *History,* published as *The Later Roman Empire, A.D. 354–378,* trans. and ed. Walter Hamilton. New York: Penguin, 1986, pp. 411–12.
10. Ammianus, *Later Roman Empire,* p. 435.
11. Gibbon, *Decline and Fall,* vol. 2, p. 512.

Chapter 2: Loss of Economic Stability and Security

12. Quoted in J.F. O'Sullivan, trans., *The Writing of Salvian the Presbyter.* Washington, DC: Catholic University of America Press, 1947, p. 140.

13. Gibbon, *Decline and Fall,* vol. 1, pp. 101–103.
14. Aelius Aristides, *Roman Panegyric,* excerpted in Naphtali Lewis and Meyer Reinhold, eds., *Roman Civilization, Sourcebook II: The Empire.* New York: Harper and Row, 1966, pp. 100, 137–38.
15. A.H.M. Jones, *Constantine and the Conversion of Europe.* Toronto: University of Toronto Press, 1979, pp. 17–18.
16. Ellsworth Huntington, "Climatic Change and Agricultural Exhaustion as Elements in the Fall of Rome," in Chambers, *Fall of the Roman Empire,* p. 55.
17. Arthur Boak and William G. Sinnegin, *A History of Rome to 565 A.D.* New York: Macmillan, 1965, pp. 455–56.
18. Quoted in Lewis and Reinhold, *Sourcebook II,* p. 437.
19. Quoted in Grant, *Fall of the Roman Empire,* p. 62.
20. Grant, *Fall of the Roman Empire,* p. 54.
21. Diocletian, *Economic Edict,* quoted in Lewis and Reinhold, *Sourcebook II,* pp. 464–72.
22. A.H.M. Jones, *The Decline of the Ancient World.* London: Longman, 1966, p. 35.
23. Quoted in Lewis and Reinhold, *Sourcebook II,* p. 477.
24. Jones, *Decline of the Ancient World,* pp. 365–66.

Chapter 3: Increasing Political and Social Disunity

25. Grant, *Fall of the Roman Empire,* p. 23.
26. Gibbon, *Decline and Fall,* vol. 1, pp. 591, 595–96.
27. Ammianus, *Later Roman Empire,* pp. 315, 317–18.
28. Jones, *Decline of the Ancient World,* pp. 362–63.
29. Quoted in O'Sullivan, *Writing of Salvian,* pp. 140–41.
30. Grant, *Fall of the Roman Empire,* p. 60.
31. Quoted in Grant, *Fall of the Roman Empire,* p. 70.
32. Ammianus, *Later Roman Empire,* pp. 46–48.
33. Harold Mattingly, *The Man on the Roman Street.* New York: W.W. Norton, 1966, p. 147.
34. Grant, *Fall of the Roman Empire,* pp. 72–73.

Chapter 4: Christianity Weakens the Roman Spirit

35. Gibbon, *Decline and Fall,* vol. 1, pp. 481–82.
36. Jones, *Decline of the Ancient World,* p. 25.
37. Jones, *Decline of the Ancient World,* p. 25.
38. Grant, *Fall of the Roman Empire,* pp. 157–58.
39. Gibbon, *Decline and Fall,* vol. 1, pp. 750–51.

40. Justo L. Gonzalez, *The Story of Christianity,* vol. 1, *The Early Church to the Dawn of the Reformation.* San Francisco: Harper and Row, 1984, p. 192.
41. Grant, *Fall of the Roman Empire,* p. 166.
42. Gonzalez, *Story of Christianity,* pp. 136–37.
43. Grant, *Fall of the Roman Empire,* p. 145.
44. Grant, *Fall of the Roman Empire,* p. 186.
45. Quoted in Alexander Roberts, trans., *A Select Library of Nicene and Post-Nicene Fathers of the Christian Church,* series II, 14 vols. Grand Rapids, MI: William B. Eerdmans, 1954, vol. 11, p. 22.
46. Quoted in Grant, *Fall of the Roman Empire,* p. 187.
47. Grant, *Fall of the Roman Empire,* p. 186.

Chapter 5: Fatal Deterioration of the Roman Army

48. Ferrill, *Fall of the Roman Empire,* p. 29.
49. Tacitus, *Agricola,* in *Tacitus: The* Agricola *and the* Germania, trans. Harold Mattingly, rev. S.A. Handford. New York: Penguin, 1970, p. 87.
50. Ferrill, *Fall of the Roman Empire,* p. 45.
51. The exact nature and chronology of Rome's frontier forts and mobile armies is still a matter of debate among historians. Some argue that the existence of a defense-in-depth strategy is uncertain because archaeological evidence for it is scanty. See, for example, Averil Cameron's *The Later Roman Empire,* A.D. 284–430. Cambridge, MA: Harvard University Press, 1993, pp. 141–43.
52. Zosimus, *Historia Nova,* trans. James J. Buchanan and Harold T. Davis. San Antonio, TX: Trinity University Press, 1967, p. 34.
53. Ferrill, *Fall of the Roman Empire,* pp. 47, 50.
54. Ferrill, *Fall of the Roman Empire,* pp. 84–85, 140.
55. Vegetius, *On the Roman Military,* excerpt in Simon Macdowall, *Late Roman Infantrymen, 236–565* A.D. London: Osprey, 1994, p. 14.
56. Grant, *Fall of the Roman Empire,* p. 38.
57. Pat Southern and Karen R. Dixon, *The Late Roman Army.* New Haven, CT: Yale University Press, 1996, p. 179.
58. Southern and Dixon, *Late Roman Army,* pp. 179–80.
59. Rutilius Namatianus, *Voyage Home to Gaul,* in J. Wight Duff and Arnold M. Duff, trans., *Minor Latin Poets.* Cambridge, MA: Harvard University Press, 1968, pp. 769, 775.

Chronology

B.C.

753

Traditional founding date for the city of Rome by the legendary figure Romulus (as computed and accepted by Roman scholars some seven centuries later).

509

The leading Roman landowners throw out their last king and establish the Roman Republic.

390

At the Allia River, north of Rome, a Roman army is routed by an invading army of Gauls. Not long afterward, the Romans abandon the army's traditional formations and begin to adopt new and more efficient organization and tactics.

265

Having gained control of the Italian Greek cities, Rome is master of the whole Italian peninsula.

264–241

The First Punic War, in which Rome defeats the maritime empire of Carthage, takes place.

218–201

Rome fights Carthage again in the Second Punic War, in which the Carthaginian general Hannibal crosses the Alps, invades Italy, and delivers the Romans one crippling defeat after another.

149–146

Rome annihilates Carthage in the Third Punic War.

118
The Romans establish a colony, Narbonne, in southern Gaul (now southern France).

58–51
Julius Caesar conquers the region of Transalpine Gaul (now central and northern France and Belgium), significantly expanding Roman dominion into Europe.

31
Octavian defeats Mark Antony and Egypt's Queen Cleopatra at Actium (in western Greece) and gains firm control of the Mediterranean world. Soon, the Senate confers on him the title of Augustus, the "revered one," and he becomes, in effect, Rome's first emperor.

ca. 30 B.C.–A.D. 180
Approximate years of the so-called Pax Romana, a period in which the Mediterranean world under the first several Roman emperors enjoys relative peace and prosperity.

12
Augustus's generals begin a three-year campaign in which they subdue much of central Germany.

A.D.
9
A Roman army of fifteen thousand men is annihilated in Germany's Teutoburg Forest, an event that forces Augustus to withdraw his troops from the recently secured German lands.

84
The Roman general Agricola invades Caledonia (Scotland) and defeats the natives at Mons Graupius.

98–117
Reign of the emperor Trajan, under whom the Roman Empire reaches its greatest size and power.

180
Emperor Marcus Aurelius dies and is succeeded by his son Commodus, marking the end of the Pax Romana and beginning of Rome's steady slide into economic and political crisis.

235–284

The Empire suffers under the strain of terrible political upheaval and civil strife, prompting later historians to call this period the Anarchy.

284

Diocletian ascends the throne and initiates sweeping political, economic, and military reforms, in effect reconstructing the Empire under a new blueprint. (Modern historians often call this new realm the Later Empire.)

307–337

Reign of the emperor Constantine I, who carries on the reforms begun by Diocletian.

313

Constantine and his eastern colleague, Licinius, issue the so-called Edict of Milan, which grants religious toleration to the formerly persecuted Christian sect.

330

Constantine founds the city of Constantinople on the Bosporus Strait, making it the capital of the eastern portion of the Empire.

361–363

Reign of the emperor Julian, a brilliant and capable individual who, in the face of Christianity's growing popularity, tries but fails to reestablish paganism as Rome's dominant religion.

ca. 370

The Huns, a savage nomadic people from central Asia, sweep into eastern Europe, pushing the Goths and other "barbarian" peoples into the northern Roman provinces.

378

The eastern emperor Valens is disastrously defeated by the Visigoths at Adrianople (in northern Greece).

395

The emperor Theodosius I dies, leaving his sons Arcadius and Honorius in control of a permanently divided Roman Empire.

ca. 407

As western Rome steadily loses control of several of its northern and western provinces, Britain falls under the sway of barbarian tribes.

410
The Visigoths briefly occupy and loot Rome.

418
The Visigoths invade Gaul, encountering little resistance.

455
The Vandals sack Rome.

476
The German-born general Odoacer demands that the emperor, the young Romulus Augustulus, step down. No new emperor takes his place and the western Roman Empire officially ceases to exist (though Rome and Italy remain prosperous for some time under barbarian rule). Meanwhile, the succession of Roman emperors continues in the eastern realm, which steadily evolves into the Byzantine Empire.

1453
The Ottoman Turks besiege, sack, and seize control of Constantinople, marking the official end of the last remnant of the Roman Empire.

1776–1788
The distinguished English historian Edward Gibbon publishes his massive and renowned *Decline and Fall of the Roman Empire,* initiating a flurry of fervid study and debate about Rome's fall that has continued unabated to the present.

For Further Reading

Books

Isaac Asimov, *The Roman Empire*. Boston: Houghton Mifflin, 1967. An excellent overview of the main events of the Empire, so precise and clearly written that even very basic readers will benefit.

Phil R. Cox and Annabel Spenceley, *Who Were the Romans?* New York: EDC Publications, 1994. An impressive, well-illustrated introduction to the Romans, presented in a question-and-answer format and aimed at basic readers.

Geraldine McCaughrean, *Roman Myths*. New York: Margaret McElderry (Macmillan), 2001. An extremely well-written introduction to Roman mythology for young people.

Don Nardo, *The Age of Augustus*. San Diego: Lucent Books, 1996. An overview of the reign and accomplishments of the man who created the Roman Empire.

Jonathan Rutland, *See Inside a Roman Town*. New York: Barnes and Noble, 1986. A very attractively illustrated introduction to major concepts of Roman civilization for basic readers.

Judith Simpson, *Ancient Rome*. New York: Time-Life Books, 1997. A beautifully illustrated overview of Roman civilization with a well-written text aimed at intermediate readers.

Internet Sources

Peter Green, "The Roman Army in Britain," 2003. www.morgue.demon.co.uk/Britannia.html. Has links to excellent descriptions of the Roman army that was essential to the Empire's survival.

History Net, "Fall of Rome: Online Articles," 2003. http://ancienthistory.about.com/cs/romefallarticles. Provides links to many online essays that discuss various aspects of Rome's fall.

History Net, "Valens and the Battle of Adrianople," 2003. http://ancient history.about.com/library/weekly/aa061901a.htm. An overview of the battle that marked the beginning of Rome's final period of decline.

Works Consulted

Major Works

Peter Brown, *The World of Late Antiquity,* A.D. *150–750.* New York: Harcourt Brace Jovanovich, 1971. An important and influential book that emphasizes the continuity of Roman life from the fifth to the sixth century.

Averil Cameron, *The Later Roman Empire,* A.D. *284–430.* Cambridge, MA: Harvard University Press, 1993. Takes the position that the crisis of the third century was only a temporary phase in an evolving imperial system.

Arther Ferrill, *The Fall of the Roman Empire: The Military Explanation.* New York: Thames and Hudson, 1986. Builds a strong case for the supposition that Rome fell mainly because its army grew increasingly less disciplined and formidable in the Empire's last two centuries.

Edward Gibbon, *The Decline and Fall of the Roman Empire.* 1776–1788. Reprint, ed. David Womersley. 3 vols. New York: Penguin, 1994. Remains the classic work on Rome's fall.

Michael Grant, *The Fall of the Roman Empire.* New York: Macmillan, 1990. Grant's main thesis is that Rome fell because of various manifestations of disunity.

———, *From Rome to Byzantium: The Fifth Century* A.D. London: Routledge, 1998. Excellent general view of Rome's last century.

A.H.M. Jones, *Constantine and the Conversion of Europe.* Toronto: University of Toronto Press, 1979. A good general overview of Constantine's world and his influence, particularly in the area of religion.

———, *The Decline of the Ancient World.* London: Longman, 1966. Note: This is a shortened version of Jones's massive and highly influential *The Later Roman Empire, 284–602.* Norman: Univer-

sity of Oklahoma Press, 1964. 3 vols. A superior synopsis of the
Later Empire.

Ramsay MacMullen, *Corruption and the Decline of Rome.* New Haven,
CT: Yale University Press, 1988. Suggests that Rome declined
mainly because the upper classes pursued their own personal ad-
vancement at the ultimate expense of the state.

———, *Roman Government's Response to Crisis, A.D. 235–337.* New
Haven, CT: Yale University Press, 1976. A worthwhile overview
of the crisis often called the Anarchy.

Stewart Perowne, *The End of the Roman World.* New York: Thomas Y.
Crowell, 1966. A commendable general overview of the Later Empire.

Justine Davis Randers-Pehrson, *Barbarians and Romans: The Birth
Struggle of Europe, A.D. 400–700.* Norman: University of Oklahoma
Press, 1983. A well-researched examination of the so-called barbarian peoples whose kingdoms gradually supplanted Roman territories.

Chester G. Starr, *Civilization and the Caesars.* New York: W.W. Norton, 1965. A respected scholar traces the changes in the lives of
individual Romans during the imperial centuries and emphasizes
how the old pagan views gave way to Christian ones.

———, *The Roman Empire, 27 B.C.–A.D. 476: A Study in Survival.*
New York: Oxford University Press, 1982. Another worthy volume by Starr, who here outlines the main events of later Roman
history and discusses some of the theories of Rome's demise.

Lynn White Jr., ed., *The Transformation of the Roman World: Gibbon's
Problem After Two Centuries.* Berkeley: University of California
Press, 1966. A fine and useful collection of essays by noted historians, each reconsidering Gibbon's views in light of later dis-
coveries.

Other Important Works

Primary Sources

Ammianus Marcellinus, *History,* published as *The Later Roman Empire,
A.D. 354–378.* Trans. and ed. Walter Hamilton. New York: Penguin,
1986.

O.M. Dalton, trans., *The Letters of Sidonius.* 2 vols. Oxford, England:
Clarendon Press, 1915.

J. Wight Duff and Arnold M. Duff, trans., *Minor Latin Poets.* Cambridge, MA: Harvard University Press, 1968.

S.Z. Ehler and J.B. Morrall, eds. and trans., *Church and State Through the Centuries.* Westminster, MD: Newman Press, 1954.

Naphtali Lewis and Meyer Reinhold, eds., *Roman Civilization, Sourcebook II: The Empire.* New York: Harper and Row, 1966.

Livy, *The History of Rome from Its Foundation,* books 1–5, published as *Livy: The Early History of Rome.* Trans. Aubrey de Sélincourt. New York: Penguin, 1971.

J.F. O'Sullivan, trans., *The Writing of Salvian the Presbyter.* Washington, DC: Catholic University of America Press, 1947.

Polybius, *The Histories.* Trans. Ian Scott-Kilvert. New York: Penguin, 1979.

Alexander Roberts, trans., *A Select Library of Nicene and Post-Nicene Fathers of the Christian Church,* series II. 14 vols. Grand Rapids, MI: William B. Eerdmans, 1954.

Suetonius, *Lives of the Twelve Caesars,* published as *The Twelve Caesars.* Trans. Robert Graves. Rev. Michael Grant. New York: Penguin, 1979.

Tacitus, *Tacitus, Agricola, in The* Agricola *and the* Germania. Trans. Harold Mattingly. Rev. S.A. Handford. New York: Penguin, 1970.

Zosimus, *Historia Nova.* Trans. James J. Buchanan and Harold T. Davis. San Antonio, TX: Trinity University Press, 1967.

Modern Sources

Arthur Boak and William G. Sinnegin, *A History of Rome to 565 A.D.* New York: Macmillan, 1965.

Peter Brown, *Power and Persuasion in Late Antiquity: Towards a Christian Empire.* Madison: University of Wisconsin Press, 1992.

J.B. Bury, *History of the Later Roman Empire, 395–565.* 2 vols. New York: Dover, 1957.

———, *Invasion of Europe by the Barbarians.* New York: W.W. Norton, 1967.

Mortimer Chambers, ed., *The Fall of the Roman Empire: Can It Be Explained?* New York: Holt, Rinehart, and Winston, 1963.

Will Durant, *Caesar and Christ: A History of Roman Civilization and of Christianity from Their Beginnings to A.D. 325.* New York: Simon and Schuster, 1944.

M.I. Finley, *The Ancient Economy.* Berkeley: University of California Press, 1985.

Walter Goffart, *Barbarians and Romans, A.D. 418–584: The Techniques of Accommodation.* Princeton, NJ: Princeton University Press, 1980.

Justo L. Gonzalez, *The Story of Christianity.* Vol. 1, *The Early Church to the Dawn of the Reformation.* San Francisco: Harper and Row, 1984.

Michael Grant, *The Climax of Rome.* New York: New American Library, 1968.

———, *Constantine the Great: The Man and His Times.* New York: Scribner's, 1994.

R.M. Haywood, *Myth of Rome's Fall.* Westport, CT: Greenwood Press, 1979.

Donald Kagan, ed., *Decline and Fall of the Roman Empire: Why Did It Collapse?* Boston: D.C. Heath, 1962.

Ferdinand Lot, *The End of the Ancient World and the Beginnings of the Middle Ages.* New York: Harper and Row, 1961.

Simon Macdowall, *Late Roman Infantrymen, 236–565 A.D.* London: Osprey, 1994.

Harold Mattingly, *The Man on the Roman Street.* New York: W.W. Norton, 1966.

John Julius Norwich, *Byzantium: The Early Centuries.* New York: Knopf, 1989.

Stewart Perowne, *Caesars and Saints: The Rise of the Christian State, A.D. 180–313.* New York: Barnes and Noble, 1962.

André Piganiol, *L'Empire Chrétien.* Paris: University Presses of France, 1972.

Michael I. Rostovtzeff, *Social and Economic History of the Roman Empire:* Oxford, England: Oxford University Press, 1957.

Pat Southern and Karen R. Dixon, *The Late Roman Army.* New Haven, CT: Yale University Press, 1996.

Chester G. Starr, *A History of the Ancient World.* New York: Oxford University Press, 1991.

Joseph Vogt, *The Decline of Rome: The Metamorphosis of Ancient Civilization.* Trans. Janet Sondheimer. London: Weidenfeld and Nicolson, 1967.

F.W. Walbank, *The Awful Revolution: The Decline of the Roman Empire in the West.* Toronto: University of Toronto Press, 1969.

Index

Picture Credits

About the Author

Classical historian Don Nardo has published many volumes about ancient Roman history and culture, including *From Founding to Fall: A History of Ancient Rome, The Age of Augustus, Women of Ancient Rome, Life of a Roman Gladiator,* and Greenhaven Press's *Encyclopedia of Greek and Roman Mythology.* Mr. Nardo also writes screenplays and teleplays and composes music. He lives in Massachusetts with his wife, Christine.